Crafting a Life

IN ESSAY, STORY, POEM

Also available by Donald M. Murray

Expecting the Unexpected
Teaching Myself—and Others—to Read and Write

Learning by Teaching
Selected Articles on Writing and Teaching

Shoptalk
Learning to Write with Writers

Crafting a Life

IN ESSAY, STORY, POEM

Donald M. Murray

BOYNTON/COOK PUBLISHERS
HEINEMANN
PORTSMOUTH, NH

Boynton/Cook Publishers
A subsidiary of Reed Elsevier Inc.
361 Hanover Street
Portsmouth, NH 03801-3912
Offices and agents throughout the world

We would like to thank those who have given their permission to include material in this book.

Murray, Donald Morison, 1924–
Crafting a life in essay, story, poem / by Donald M. Murray.
p. cm.
Includes bibliographical references.
ISBN 0-86709-403-6 (alk. paper)
1. English language—Rhetoric. 2. Essay—Authorship. 3. Creative writing. I. Title
PE1408.M788 1996
808'.02—dc20 96-3819
CIP

Consulting Editor: Thomas Newkirk
Production: Renée Le Verrier
Cover photos: Courtesy Donald Murray, Barbara Werden
Cover design: Barbara Werden
Manufacturing: Louise Richardson

Printed in the United States of America on acid-free paper
7 8 9 10 -DAP- 04 03 02 01

For all who have helped me craft a writing life,
especially Minnie Mae, Chip, Don, Elizabeth

Contents

Acknowledgments

I WANT TO ACKNOWLEDGE MY DEBT TO ALL THE MEMBERS OF THE WRITING communities who have helped me learn to write over the years. During the writing of this book I was particularly aware of the colleagueship of Don Graves, who is always just a phone call or a FAX away, Lisa Miller, Ralph Fletcher, Tom Romano, and Linda Buchanan Allen. I am also grateful to the always-helpful members of my poetry group and want to express appreciation to three editors—Laurie Runion, Evelynne Kramer, and Louise Kennedy—who have been both teachers and encouragers of writing.

The final draft of this book is much better than the first draft because of the insightful critical comments of Mike Angelotti, Elizabeth Cooke, Brock Dethier, Beverly LePage, Chip Scanlan, and my wife, Minnie Mae, who is always my first reader. I am grateful to the editors, artists, and production experts at Heinemann-Boynton/Cook who have collaborated in making this book, especially Toby Gordon, Scott Mahler, Renée Le Verrier, and Barbara Werden.

Tom Newkirk—friend, neighbor, colleague—made a major contribution to this book at its conception and later became the editor who saw the book within my draft that I did not see, and expressed more faith in the book than I did. It would not have been written without him.

Introduction

Why I Write

Perhaps in the beginning I wrote to get attention. I was an only child, given to behaviors that would probably now be described as hyperactive. H. L. Mencken said the writer's "...overpowering impulse is to gyrate before his fellow man, flapping his wings and emitting defiant yells. This being forbidden by the police of all civilized countries, he takes it out by putting his yells on paper. Such is the thing called self-expression." Of course, Mencken wrote before we were gender sensitive. We now know that female writers often gyrate as well. And in addition to flapping my wings, I have written to be hired by newspapers and written not to be fired (although that didn't work on *Time* magazine). I have certainly written for money, freelancing fulltime when our children were young and we were all hungry.

I began to write long before I could read, even before I could print my name—even before I was born. We lived with my grandmother, who told me stories of Scotland and coming to America. I was brought up in a house of narrative. I was told stories of moral instruction. I also overheard stories I was not supposed to hear by sneaking out of bed and lying on the cold winter floor, my ear to the open grate that allowed heat—and stories—to rise to the second floor. I don't remember when I could not read. I entered the page to serve with Robin Hood, Long John Silver, Rob Roy and as a Knight of the Round Table. We were hard-shell Baptists, and I was instructed by parables. The Bible was a story about stories.

In this good Christian home that a social worker might now describe as "dysfunctional" I not only received stories, I made them up. I can remember stories I told myself to explain the swirling cross-currents of love and guilt, control and anxiety in every house in which we lived—and I can retell the stories I told to escape. I had a secret family who lived in the wall, and a ceiling covered with *National Geographic* maps.

Of course I did not escape my family—none of us does—but I still tell myself—and now others—the stories I need to create and recreate, to celebrate and understand the life I have lived. Catherine Drinker Bowen once wrote, "Writing, I think, is not apart from living. Writing is a kind of double living. The writer experiences everything twice. Once in reality and once in that mirror which waits always before or behind him." I have lived my life not once, but a hundred times in night dreams and day dreams, in imaginings and fantasy, in the essays, stories, poems I have told myself—and my readers.

I can not believe my good fortune in being able, through story, to live a life of memory and imagination—leaving the dinner party, the lecture, concert, book, TV show, drive in the car, the conversation—to enter that other life, and each morning to slide into that bubble of quiet concentration where the page tells me what I didn't know I knew, as I weave still another life.

As I pass into my seventies, friends advise me to escape the weekly column and book deadlines, to be relieved of the obsessive compulsion to put more words on paper and count them every day, to make up more stories, more poems; but writing is not my punishment, it is my delight. And yet, I suppose, I should take account and try to identify the reasons I set the alarm for 5:30 A.M. but often rise before it goes off, eager to get to the desk where I craft my life.

I Write to Say I Am

When I write, I create myself, and that created self, through writing, may affect the world. As Anita Brookner said, "I started writing because of a terrible feeling of powerlessness: I felt I was drifting and obscure, and I rebelled against that. I didn't see what I could do to change my condition. I wanted to control rather than be controlled, to ordain rather than be ordained, and to relegate rather than be relegated."

Most of us feel invisible. We are not seen. We wait on tables and the diners do not see us, talking about us as if we did not exist. When we write we become visible, we are players in the game of life. We—our writings—have to be dealt with. It is far more difficult, unfortunately, to ignore a memo, argument, proposal, published article, than it is to ignore a human being.

The ability to collect and organize information, discover its significance and make that available to others, gives the writer significance. Through writing the writer can influence and persuade. The writer becomes a presence, existing in a way that he or she does not when silent.

I Write to Discover Who I Am

Of course I began writing to become what I was not. When we are young we try on roles; I wanted to escape my skin and become Ernest Hemingway, Kenneth Roberts, Jack London, Robert Louis Stevenson, Willa Cather. But soon I learned that writing reveals—always. Wynton Marsallis explains, "You can't play different from who you are." I wrote, and there was Don Murray on the page.

The fear of exposure by writing is a rational fear. But in the act of exposure, writers discover themselves. I meet myself on the page and after decades of writing I have come to accept myself—I'd better—and in the process of writing I have learned who I am—and have found a person with whom I can live and work, a person I keep needing to rediscover.

More than that, I have discovered my strengths are my differences. Difference is a terrible thing to a child. I hungered for acceptance, to conform, but part of me always stood apart, at the edge of the playground. My imagined or reflected life—my ability to enter the skins of others, my need to construct stories, my compulsion to live in books as much as on the street, my habit of daydreaming, my need to connect, my delight in contradiction, my love affair with language—I always thought a weakness, and so did my parents and most of my teachers. But these "weaknesses" have paid my bills and, more importantly, the opportunity to develop my "weaknesses" through writing has given me a blessed life.

Write to Create Your Life

Becoming myself, I become others. When Flaubert was asked who Madame Bovary was he answered, "C'est moi." And Hortense Calisher said, "The novel is rescued life."

This mysterious and enriching process is demonstrated in a poem of mine.

THE OTHER LIFE

My mother imagined an only child,
sold my unnamed twin for folded
cash, never told my father why
his son came home alone. My twin
lived in Iowa and I was sure
he knew the secret of airedales,
how to get oatmeal globs down
his throat, was not afraid

when water rose above his head.
Liked school, could pole vault,
lived in a single family house,
knew his parents wanted him.

During my muddy war he braced
his feet against Pacific swells
on a destroyer, later studied art
in New York City, Paris, Florence,

has lived in San Francisco 34 years
with a printer named George. My twin
is lean, bald, but with a beard.
He rides a racing bike, plays bassoon,

high stake poker every other Thursday
night, adopted a walrus at the Aquarium.
Each day he draws fewer lines, watches
as they reveal more, imagines his twin.

Until I wrote the poem I did not have a twin, but I do now.

When writing we do not leave ourselves but extend ourselves. In a novel I became a person paralyzed from the neck down; in nonfiction articles I became the United States Secretary of Labor, a mental patient, the New York Police Commissioner, a world-famous classical violinist, a woman alcoholic, an orthopedic surgeon.

I Write to Understand My Life

Joan Didion says, "Had I been blessed with even limited access to my own mind there would have been no reason to write. I write entirely to find out what I'm thinking, what I'm looking at, what I see and what it means. What I want and what I fear." I write this book and others to learn as much as I can about the magic I have always found on the page. I write my weekly newspaper columns to understand my aging; my novel to understand my war; my poems to understand the images, memories, and fragments of language that have the power to illuminate my world.

I Write to Slay My Dragons

During the past year, I suffered short periods—measured by hours, not days—from a depression or unexpected terror that seemed both physical and mental. The attacks were sudden and frightening. I had never suffered from depression before and suspected the attacks were caused by a drug I was taking. Prescriptions were changed but I did not escape the fears that lay in ambush.

I did, however, remember Donald Barthelme's advice to "Write about what you're most afraid of." When I was able to force myself to write, my internal enemy would retreat.

Now I have some emergency pills that help relieve the depression—and therapy that has made the pills—but not the writing—less important. If I write, the dark shadows move away from my desk. Telling myself stories was my comfort in my childhood and in combat. In the hours between my heart attack and my by-pass operation, I dictated a column to Minnie Mae, who understood I didn't write so much out of a compulsive obsession with productivity instead to name and therefore defeat the dragon that waited, snorting flaming bad breath, in the operating room.

I Write to Exercise My Craft

I find joy in learning my craft and comfort now that I am old enough to know I will never stop learning to write. Each year I better understand the Japanese artist Hokusai who said, "I have drawn things since I was six. All that I made before the age of sixty-five is not worth counting. At seventy-three I began to understand the true construction of animals, plants, trees, birds, fishes, and insects. At ninety I will enter into the secret of things. At a hundred and ten, everything—every dot, every dash—will live."

I am happiest when I am rubbing two words together to produce an unexpected insight, when I feel the sentence turn under my hand, the paragraph shrink or rise until it breaks in two, the narrative flow toward rapids I can hear but do not yet see. The draft is always, for me, alive with possibility. The task may seem routine, even dreary, as I approach it;

but once I am in the act of writing it makes its own demand and carries me along on another adventure in meaning.

I spend my mornings messing around in language, learning the rules and then breaking them, making up words, listening to the beat and melody of language, putting in and taking out, fitting and shaping, moving and removing, playing language into meaning.

I Write to Lose Myself in My Work

"If it is winter in the book, spring surprises me when I look up," said Bernard Malamud, who knew that concentration is one of the great healing gifts of writing. When I am within a draft, I escape the headlines, the family crisis, the distractions of life around me. I write to music—this chapter was drafted to Bach's *B Minor Mass,* revised to Mozart's *Twenty-second Piano Concerto,* revised once more to Stravinsky's *Pulcinella Suite*—but when the writing goes well, the music is unheard and when I am interrupted I can return to this place within the writing that absorbs all my senses, all my thoughts and emotions, all my energy. These quiet moments of craft are the anchor to my life.

I Write for Revenge

I reacted so violently against the statement of John Hawks that "Fiction is an act of revenge" that I realized he had found me out. I write in retaliation against the family that thought I was ugly and strange, against the teachers who said I was stupid, against the officers who sent me into battle.

I Write to Share

The writing act is an escape from loneliness. I need aloneness to write, to read, to think, to imagine, but I also need to escape this necessary loneliness—after the writing is done. Heather McHugh described one reason I write when she said, "I began to write because I was too shy to talk, and too lonely not to send messages."

I am surprised and nurtured by the reaction of my readers. Books are years in the making and I may never meet a reader even after they are published, but one of the pleasures of column writing is that strangers, acquaintances, neighbors, and friends respond to columns within hours of publication.

And when I am willing to write about the most private things—the memory of the daughter we lost, how easy it was to pull the trigger when an enemy was in my rifle sight—I get the most reader response. We forge communities when we share who we are, what we feel, what we think; and writing allows a sharing beyond the room, even beyond our lifetime. The best writing often rises out of loneliness, but it is a momentary escape from loneliness or, in a way, a celebration of loneliness. By sharing our solitude we come both to respect it and to create a door that allows us to leave and return to the essential loneliness from which so much writing comes.

I Write to Testify

I may not stand up in Wednesday-night prayer meeting, but I have not escaped the Baptist tradition of giving testimony. Elie Wiesel speaks of the importance of his bearing witness to the Holocaust: "Writing is a duty for me as a survivor. I entered literature through silence; I seek the role of witness, and I am duty bound to justify each moment of my life as a survivor." I also bear witness to the horrors of war, to the shame of describing a child who learns differently from others as "stupid," to the wonder of my unexpected life. We can bear witness *for* as well as *against*. And as writers, we can do it without taking to the streets. Emily Dickinson gave witness from her secluded life in Amherst, Massachusetts. All writers have an obligation to testify what they have witnessed and to testify how they have survived.

I write about war because I think it is the duty of old soldiers who have survived infantry combat—where death and injury often come from flying body parts—to tell those who make wars about the realities of combat. I bear witness to how it feels to do badly in school, what it is like to have a child die before I do, how it feels to be old. We all need to tell our stories and our stories need to be heard.

I Write to Avoid Boredom

Since leaving school, I don't think I have ever been bored. When Gish Jen was asked why she wrote, she said, "I think I'm trying to keep myself from being bored. When I think about why I would be a writer, why I should continue to be a writer, it seems to me one of the few things you can do where you're never bored."

I write about the world in which I live, my external and internal life, finding as I write that the most trivial events have meaning. Writing instructs me about the life I live. And if I ever am bored, I will write an essay on boredom.

I Write to Celebrate

To celebrate means to respect, and all my writing is a celebration of life. Writing makes me aware of the extraordinary in the ordinary. Writing increases the texture of my life and my appreciation of that texture. Colors are bright, smells more flavorful, sounds—even the sounds of silence—are stronger when I write them down. Writing increases memory and awareness. I am most alive when I am writing. As the artist Louise Nevelson said, "My work is a feast for myself."

1

Before Writing

Give Yourself Permission to Write

There is no censorship in the world as powerful as self-censorship. Many of us hunger to write, need to experience our world once in reality and then to understand it through the insights of art, seeing with words what we had not seen at the moment of experience, discovering patterns that reveal meaning in experience. We need to write and to be read.

Writing is not a turning away from life but a turning toward life, a way of extending the experience. Catherine Drinker Bowen explained, "Writing, I think, is not apart from living. Writing is a kind of double living. The writer experiences everything twice. Once in reality and once in that mirror which waits always before or behind him." Those of us who are readers of books and of life, imaginers, make believers, players with language, censor this need only at great risk.

Writers Who Don't Write

Most writers never write. They want to be writers. They intend to write this weekend or next, on Monday or the following Monday, on summer vacation or winter vacation, when the kids start school or graduate from college, when they retire and have more free time. They *are* writers in that they tell themselves the story of their lives, see their lives in a writerly way: recording images, fragments of conversations, observation of what is and what should be, making connections, making story from chaos.

They read other writers and tell themselves they have a story as powerful as the published writers'. They imagine writing, perhaps even preparing an office—Virginia Woolf's "room of one's own." They buy books and magazines on writing, sign up for workshops and courses, store up reams of paper or megabytes of hard-disk space for the writing they intend to produce; but the page remains blank.

These writers who don't write do have talent, voices, insight, stories to tell that we need to hear. They could perform the writer's task of articulating our fears, hopes, anxieties, joys, terrors, knowledge. We would be richer by their speaking, but they remain silent, and their silence is their loss—and ours.

Writers Who Don't Finish

Many others write but do not finish what they start. They write brilliant fragments, anecdotes, scenes, character sketches, lines of poetry, first pages of essays, forewords to books, openings of short stories and novels, journal notes—but not finished essays, stories, poems.

They open but they do not close. The writers who do not finish have discovered the magic of language, know the truth of what Wallace Stevens said: "The tongue is an eye." They have written what they did not expect to write, discovering how writing develops and changes their experience. But they faced writing problems they believed they could not solve, so they stopped writing. They did not have the commitment of a contract, the blessing of a deadline, pressure from a waiting editor or hungry children, as I did when I was free lancing full-time, to force them to write without faith in themselves.

These writers have drawers and file cabinets full of grand beginnings, centers without beginnings or endings, endings that could not attach themselves to a start. The writers who do not finish—and those who do not write—make up the great majority of all writers.

Writers Who Don't Submit for Publication

Some writers complete what they start but do not submit their writing for publication. They do not know how to approach an editor or an agent. They anticipate failure, rejecting themselves before an editor has a chance to do it. They never mail their manuscripts, or only mail things out once or twice before quitting. (These writers may not believe the stories of famous writers whose stories, poems, and books were rejected twenty, thirty, fifty times before they were accepted.)

When I taught writing, my greatest complaint was not that my students couldn't write—they could—but that they didn't. They had important stories to tell, but often the most talented students who had the most important stories to tell simply didn't finish them—or when they did, didn't send them out for publication. They censored themselves.

College professors make the same complaints although they are given time to publish and, in fact, are required to do so. Yet, a few years ago a major journal in the field of composition theory and pedagogy had only eight rejected articles for one issue because so few had been submitted.

When I worked as a writing coach for newspapers, reporters complained to me that they didn't get the best assignments—but their best stories usually stayed in their notebooks. They did not write and submit them, knowing they would be rejected. But when I could convince them to write their real stories and show them to their editors, the stories were usually published. As a young newspaperman myself, I was told that the *Boston Herald* would not publish stories critical of a Republican administration; yet when I wrote editorials on military affairs that were extremely critical of a Republican administration, the *Herald* published them and I was awarded a Pulitzer prize.

I was told that first-person, anecdotal articles could not be published in academic journals. I submitted such articles and they were published. And yet I still commit self-censorship after all these years, not sending out poems and stories I have written, or putting them away after one or two rejections. I have to keep teaching myself how to overcome self-censorship.

The reasons we don't write are personal—and universal. At the same time, we feel we have something important to say and nothing important to say: Checkmate. We don't think anyone will listen, a feeling often reinforced during our childhood and into professional life. This feeling of not being heard is greater for women than for men, and greater for members of racial and ethnic groups that are not part of the political-economic power structure. But all of us question our talent, our creativity, our ability to write well enough to earn a reader's attention.

Writers' Excuses

"I don't have anything worth saying." This may be true, but you won't know what you have to say until you write. The draft itself reveals what you know that you didn't know you knew. Many of my students have gone on to become professionals who publish poetry, articles and nonfiction books, children's books, short stories, and novels. Few of these writers were the *most* talented in my classes. Some were even among the least talented.

I gave one student a *B*-minus with the promise he would not take another writing class. Later, he enjoyed sending me announcements of grants and awards he had won for his writing. Another student who did poorly in my class and actually flunked a colleague's writing class, enjoyed visiting us after she won a Pulitzer.

"Nothing very dramatic has happened to me." Nonsense. We may not value our own experience, but we have lived a life of pleasure and dread, loss and recovery, the solemn and the ridiculous. Writing may come, as some of mine does, from the terrible experience of life—the death of a daughter, survival under shellfire—but most of it comes from wonder at the ordinary—a grandson's first step, a turn of the season, an hour in a hospital waiting room. Writing comes from paying attention.

"I don't live in Manhattan or Hollywood." Good. The best writing is not born over lunch between publishers and movie makers, but from ordinary human beings far away from those cities who write of the worlds they find within themselves. As Herman Melville said, "It is not down in any map: true places never are." Annie Dillard, Barbara Kingsolver, Diane Ackerman, Barry Lopez, and many other fine writers have respected—celebrated—what seemed to be local, ordinary, familiar, insignificant until their writing revealed its universality.

"No one would be interested in what I have to say." The brilliant young novelist Alice McDermott says, "The hardest thing I had to do even to become a writer was believing that I had anything to say that people would want to read." We all feel this way. I was trained under the rule that "Children should be seen and not heard." We were shushed and not listened to; our opinions were not taken seriously, especially the girls. School was a place where we listened to the teacher who did not listen to us. As adults now, we discover that many people will be interested in what we say only if we have the courage to write something personal and share it. Then readers will respond.

"I'm not talented." Talent in writing is common. I've worked with elementary-school students, and they all are talented—even many pupils who are tracked as "slow"—until the fourth grade when society, school, hormones start to convince some children they are not talented. But talent can be revealed by writing when you are twenty, fifty, eighty and beyond. Each class I taught, at every level, was loaded with talent—the potential to accomplish something. I always believed the majority of my students were more talented than I was, certainly at their age. But they would probably not develop or hone the talent they had.

"I'm not creative." Writers hate that word. Creativity implies originality, work that calls attention to itself, work that is eccentric only to be eccentric. Writers do not tell new stories, they tell the old stories in their own individual way. There is little true originality in art. The writer should focus on revealing, as simply and clearly as possible.

"I will expose myself if I write." Yes. But we also reveal ourselves if we remain silent. Blank pages as well as the written pages are a testimony to how we live our lives. The first person to whom you reveal yourself by writing is yourself. You are your own reader and as you write what you do not expect to write, you will discover who you are, what your world is like, and what your life means.

"I don't have time to write." Nobody has time to write, but writers find the time as do joggers, quilters, lovers, golfers. Writers write; in the next chapter we will discuss how most of them find the time.

"I don't know how to write." I should hope not. Writing is a lifetime apprenticeship to the word. You'll never know exactly how to write the next piece. If you do, you'll write what you have written before. You will always be learning to write—that is the blessing of craft.

"I'm too old to learn to write." Youth is an advantage to a ballet dancer or a basketball player, but it is a disadvantage to a writer. The writer needs distance from experience, and the young writer does not yet have that. Harriet Doerr left college before graduating and published *Stones from Ibarra* when she was seventy-three and won the American Book Award for First Fiction the next year. It helps as a writer to see childhood from the distance of a parent, the job from the perspective of one who has lost a job. Age brings us the many levels of vision we need in order to write. We know health and illness, joy and sadness, belief and doubt. We need the blend of thought and feelings, memories and imaginings, caught and mixed together by words and the pauses between words that flow toward significance.

"If I finished something I wouldn't know what to do with it." It takes a certain need or arrogance to publish and, in my case, I needed the help of a young woman I met. I was working at a newspaper when I met

Minnie Mae. I admitted to her that I wanted to publish magazine articles and confessed I had even written some, but was so critical of them that I used them to start fires in my fireplace. Minnie Mae started sending them off before we were married and they were published after the wedding.

"I hate what I write." That is natural. What appears on the page is rarely what we expect or want to see. But that is the nature of art. Life is transformed in the act of making; our children become themselves and so do our drafts. We have been taught not to respect ourselves, not to be different, not to confront our secret selves, but this is the writer's task: to be oneself. When the Prince Regent's librarian wrote Jane Austen, asking her to write a romance, she wrote back: "No, I must keep to my own style, and go on in my own way; and though I may never succeed *again* in that, I am convinced that I should totally fail in any other." She went on to write *Persuasion.*

"I have responsibilities to other people." When I first arrived at the University of New Hampshire, some aggressively publishing faculty members—all male—scorned teaching and family responsibilities as "virtuous evasions" of publishing. I admit that I often felt guilty when I left the writing desk to fulfill other responsibilities, then I decided that if I had to trade "good writer" for "good husband," "good father and grandfather," "good teacher," "good friend," so be it. But you don't. Most of us can find a few minutes alone at the beginning or at the end of the day—or in cracks of time during the middle—for ourselves. And we will be better at all our other roles in life if we fulfill the responsibilities we have to ourselves.

"But now what do I do?" Many of us also fear that the dream will come true. We imagine that a teacher or an editor will say we can write, but when they do the stakes go up; we no longer have the excuse of inadequacy and that can be terrifying. But you must still put one word on paper and then another word, and another. William Faulkner said of writing fiction, "It begins with a character, usually, and once he stands up on his feet and begins to move, all I do is trot along behind him with a paper and pencil trying to keep up long enough to put down what he says and does." Give yourself permission to trot along behind your sentences, living the greater reality of the written life.

Cultivating a Writing Habit

Wait for inspiration to write . . .
and you will never be published.

For writers, the act of writing becomes a habit, a ritual, a discipline, a compulsion. The most effective form of inspiration rarely occurs during the writing. We think by writing. As Joan Didion says, "I write entirely to find out what I'm thinking, what I'm looking at, what I see and what it means. What I want and what I fear."

Annie Dillard puts the necessary discipline in an appropriate context:

> There's a common notion that self-discipline is a freakish peculiarity of writers—that writers differ from other people by possessing enormous and equal portions of talent and willpower. They grit their powerful teeth and go into their little rooms. I think that's a bad misunderstanding of what impels the writer. What impels the writer is a deep love for and respect for language, for literary forms, for books. It's a privilege to muck about in sentences all morning. It's a challenge to bring off a powerful effect. You don't do it from willpower; you do it from an abiding passion for the field. I'm sure it's the same in every other field.
>
> Writing a book is like rearing children—willpower has very little to do with it. If you have a little baby crying in the middle of the night, and if you depend only on willpower to get you out of bed to feed the baby, that baby will starve. You do it out of love. Willpower is a weak idea; love is strong. You don't have to scrouge yourself with cat-o'-nine tails to go to the baby. You go to the baby out of love for that particular baby. That's the same way you go to your desk. There's nothing freakish about it. Caring passionately about something isn't against nature, and it isn't against human nature. It's what we're here to do.

The reason I continue to write is not so much for publication, for fame, for money, but for surprise. And in surprise, understanding; and, in understanding, healing. I write and learn. I write against my own intent, saying what I do not expect to say, and discover the shape and texture and meaning of the world in which I live. My writing is a celebration—sometimes painful, more often joyful—of the life I am leading. *But it will not happen without my morning habit of writing.*

The reader should beware. I will discuss my writing habits but I have no loyalty to specific ones. They will change with new writing projects, age, family situation, health, experience, and emotions.

Try my writing routine on for size if you want to; but I am *not* suggesting it should be your writing routine. Many productive writers have habits different from mine. Most productive writers write daily as I do, but there are binge writers. I get up at 5:30 A.M. and write—most writers rise early and write early—but some writers start when the rest of the world goes to bed. The important thing is not *how* you write but *if* you write. Prolific mystery writer Robert B. Parker explains:

> There is no one right way. Each of us finds a way that works for him. But there is a wrong way. The wrong is to finish your day with no more words on paper than when you began. Writers write. Your own habits should grow out of your own personality, thinking and working styles, writing tasks and environment.

Rosellen Brown agrees:

> It's a job. It's not a hobby. You don't write the way you build a model airplane. You have to sit down and work, to schedule your time and stick to it. Even if it's just for an hour or so each day, you have to get a babysitter and make the time. If you're going to make writing succeed you have to approach it as a job. You don't wait for inspiration. The muse does not do your work for you.

Graham Greene says:

> If one wants to write, one simply has to organize one's life in a mass of little habits.

Here are my little habits. Your own habits should grow out of your own personality, thinking and working styles, writing tasks and environment.

My writing day begins when I click off the computer at about 11:30 in the morning. I try to write only in the morning and leave my desk without having drained the well on a long project. My newspaper column is drafted, revised, edited and finished in a morning—after a week of conscious and unconscious awareness and rehearsal.

I Talk to Myself

Professor Donald Graves' research in young children documented the importance of rehearsal for writing. The students who wrote most easily and most effectively had been talking to themselves, telling the story consciously and subconsciously before writing.

E. B. White said:

> Delay is natural to a writer. He is like a surfer—he bides his time, waits for the perfect wave on which to ride in. Delay is instinctive with him. He waits for the surge (of emotion? of strength? of courage?) that will carry him along.

Virginia Woolf wrote:

> As for my next book, I am going to hold myself from writing it till I have it impending in me: grown heavy in my mind like a ripe pear; pendant, gravid, asking to be cut or it will fall.

Ripeness for me is when the writing comes easily, flowing on its own tide. This must be explored in writing. Now. Today. This morning. Many times this writing elbows its way into my consciousness when I am writing something else and I must attend to it, writing at least enough to capture an idea, a voice, a structure so I can return to it later.

I Set Deadlines

Ripeness is a product of a deadline. Without a deadline I do not begin to write and finish what I am writing. I have yearly, monthly, and weekly deadlines but the most important one is tomorrow morning's deadline. All day—and night—long I know I am going to attend to the ending of an article, the beginning of a chapter, the sketching of a scene, the drafting of a poem.

I Write Every Day

There are a few words that are framed above the clock over my desk, encased in a plastic sign on the bookcase behind my computer monitor, sewn in needle point and framed on the wall to my left, encased in hard plastic beside my keyboard

nulla dies sine linea

Horace, Pliny, Trollope, Updike and many others have followed this fundamental rule: *Never a day without a line.* The writing muscle must be exercised. If we are not in the habit of receiving writing, none will be delivered.

I Break Projects into Achievable Daily Tasks

Years ago I saw an interview with the first woman climber to scale a rock face in California. She had to spend days and nights in a sling on a rock face, inching her way up. When she made it they asked her how she did it and she answered, "You eat an elephant a bite at a time." I adopted her bite-at-a-time method to write my books.

John Steinbeck said:

> When I face the desolate impossibility of writing 500 pages a sick sense of failure falls on me and I know I can never do it. Then gradually I write one page and then another. One day's work is all I can permit myself to contemplate.

I break each writing project into small, achievable tasks: brainstorm to narrow topic, write a discovery draft, draft leads, finish scene, revise poem, edit chapter, outline new textbook, play with war poem. The important thing for me is not to make the description global—write war novel—or impossible to achieve in a morning—write entire work habit chapter tomorrow morning. Instead, I tell myself to begin the scene in the ravine or write the lead and outline for Chapter 3.

Keep Score

Many writers—Faulkner, Hemingway, and others—counted the words they wrote each day. As an elderly man, Graham Greene said, " . . . In the old days, at the beginning of a book, I'd set myself five hundred words a day, but now I'd put the mark to about three hundred words."

I have often counted words. In fact, I have a record of exactly how many words I wrote every day for the entire decade of the 1970s, a time when I was heavily involved in teaching, consulting, speaking, administration, and campus politics. To get one draft of a book written I set the goal at three hundred words (one page) a day. Some days I wrote less, some days I wrote more, and some days I stared at a blank page; but the draft got written.

I count words to avoid the question of quality, especially on a book. If I ask myself, "How well did I write today?" I despair and may even abandon the book. If I ask myself, "How much did I write today?" I can answer "311 words" or "27 words" or a heroic "1,103 words." I avoid the question of quality, which cannot be answered until the book is done. If you count words and miss a day, do not add that word count goal to the next day. I used to do that. If the goal was three hundred words a morning and I missed, I'd make the next day six hundred and soon I had a nine-hundred–word goal and when I put down a heroic 657 words, I would feel that I had a bad writing day.

Other times I have kept a record of the hours I have spent writing, even using a stop-watch to time myself. That time count reinforced my belief that true productivity results from brief, daily writing rather than from heroic, infrequent bursts of writing. At the moment I am simply establishing at least one writing task every day and completing it—and maybe one more.

I Know Tomorrow Morning's Task Tonight

I am promiscuous—as a writer. I take on too many projects and try to split my writing mornings into two or three tasks—the column, this book, the novel, a poem, an article. It doesn't work. Each night I write down tomorrow's single writing task on a card, assigning the writing to my subconscious, where most of the writing gets done.

I Write in the Morning

My writing day ends when I write—twenty or so hours of rehearsal, culminating in an hour or so of writing in the morning. I have studied the work habits of thousands of writers and most of them write in the morning when they can draw from their subconscious before the world intrudes. In retirement I set the clock alarm for 5:30 A.M. but often get up earlier, itching to get to my writing desk. I can't, however, leap from bed into a paragraph. I read the paper, drink my juice, take my pills, meet cronies at the Bagelry, take my walk and get to my desk at about 7:30 A.M. awake and ready to write.

I have found that ninety minutes is my ideal writing time, broken into ten- or fifteen-minute bursts. (I might get one thirty-minute burst.) But I need an envelope of time around those moments of writing: ninety minutes often takes three hours.

I try never to write after lunch, in the afternoon or the evening although I am writing this at 4:24 P.M. Rules are meant to be broken. But I write better if I allow the well to fill in the afternoon and evening.

I Stop Before I Finish

On long projects, I quit before I get to the end of what I have to say. If I drain the well it refills very slowly and may not contain enough writing for me to draw on the next day. I do my stint and stop when I still have a hint of what may come next. Sometimes I will scribble a note to myself: "Define fluency" or "Blair leaves hospital."

I Have a Room of My Own

I can still place myself in my first writing room—a closet with a small window in the room where my grandmother lay paralyzed. I built a desk with boards placed on orange crates. It was my study, my comfort and my delight.

Now I have a large room with a wall of patio doors facing our woods. Many writers sit with their backs to the view, but I like to look up and enjoy the seasons. I have a large collection of compact disks and work as I studied in high school, with music playing. Then it was mostly swing; now it is mostly classical.

I work surrounded by an electronics shipping plant: computer, photocopier, fax machine, disk backup, scanner, modem, printer, telephone, hi fi system behind me, a small color TV on the shelf ahead. And books, of course, books on shelves and books stacked in front of the shelves, and six file cabinets under my giant "L" of working surface. And pictures of my grandchildren, Sienna, the Norwegian Arctic night, a salt marsh.

I Have Favorite Tools

I am obsessive about the pens—black, fine point—that I use to write and to sketch. I always have three pens in my shirt pocket, together with a leather case that has 3" x 5" cards on which I can make notes, and recently I have been carrying a small sketchbook as well.

I have a canvas case that goes almost everywhere with me and that contains other writing tools, and my daybook, a spiral, 8" x 10" notebook with thin lines and green tinted paper. I am just finishing daybook #92.

I plan and outline, note and predraft in my daybook, in which I paste pages printed out from my computer that I may want to edit, quotes from writers, pictures, poems, whatever helps in the conversation I carry on with myself about what and how I write. I call it a daybook because when I call it a journal I begin to write pompous blather. In the daybook or log, I do not philosophize; it is a workbook similar to what a scientist might have in a lab. I write on a large, fast desktop computer in my office and keep the laptop I take on trips beside my chair upstairs so I can use it as a notebook.

Some Tricks of My Trade

When interrupted. I come from a city-room background and don't mind a few phone calls during a writing morning, even a couple of faxes. In fact, I find it more efficient to take phone calls than to let the answering machine collect messages that take a dozen calls to answer. When I am interrupted, I immediately punch the save-to-floppy-disk keys and I stop in the middle of a sentence because it will be easy to get back into the writing by finishing the sentence. For example: "And I stop in the middle of a sentence because [. . . INTERRUPTION . . .] it will be easy to get back into the writing by finishing the sentence."

I treasure some of the interruptions. Colleagues Don Graves and Chip Scanlan often interrupt my morning work—and I interrupt theirs. We are toiling at similar workbenches and I find our gossip stimulating and supportive. Yet I battle the larger interruptions of morning appointments, meetings and interruptions from strangers. In the morning I make no dental or doctor's appointments, do not schedule car repairs, try never to socialize. In my office is a statement by Charles Dickens:

> "It is only half-an-hour"—"It is only an afternoon"—"It is only an evening," people say to me over and over again; but they don't know that it is impossible to command one's self sometimes to any stipulated and set disposal of five minutes—or that the mere consciousness of an engagement will sometimes worry a whole day.

When stuck. I back off, work on a different project, return later. If I am doing a book, I often jump ahead to the next section within a chapter, return later to find the problem solved. I do not force the writing but create an emotional and intellectual environment that will allow me to hear and accept the writing.

Creating Your Own Writing Habit

Look to when the writing went well. Study how you wrote when the writing came easily. The old adage, "Easy writing makes hard reading" is simply not true. Easy writing makes easy reading. Ask yourself:

- Where did I get the idea?
- What did I do with it?
- What planning, drafting, revising and editing techniques worked?
- What process did I use to take the project from idea to completion?

- Whom did I share a draft with or discuss a problem with during the process?
- Who helped me?
- How?
- What tools did I use? How did they help?
- Where did I write it?
- What environmental conditions helped—background music, view, furniture?
- How much time did I take?
- How close to deadline did I work?
- Whom did I deliver it to?
- What did he or she do that helped?
- What was different from how I usually work?

Ask any other questions and then attempt to replicate the conditions as you write. After you have found one successful way to work, you will be able to adapt it to new tasks and different conditions. Your writing habit will evolve as you become a more experienced writer.

But remember, if you want to write, the rump has to meet the chair on schedule. The rear end is the writing muscle that makes the difference between the writers who want to write and don't, and those writers who want to write and do.

You may not be able to achieve the enormous writing habit of Anthony Trollope—and may not even want to, but for decades the following statement from him has hung on my study wall:

> As I journeyed across France and Marseilles, and made thence a terribly rough voyage to Alexandria, I wrote my allotted number of pages every day. On this occasion more than once I left my paper on the cabin table, rushing away to be sick in the privacy of my stateroom. It was February, and the weather was miserable; but still I did my work.
>
> It has . . . become my custom . . . to write with my watch before me, and to require from myself 250 words every quarter of an hour. I have found that the 250 words have been forthcoming as regularly as my watch went.
>
> There are those who would be ashamed to subject themselves to such a taskmaster, and who think that the man who works with his imagination should allow himself to wait till inspiration moves him . . . To me it would not be more absurd if the shoemaker were to wait for inspiration, or the tallow-chandler for the divine moment of melting . . .

> A man can always do the work for which his brain is fitted if he will give himself the habit of regarding his work as a normal condition of his life. I therefore venture to advise young men who look forward to authorship as the business of their lives, even when they propose that authorship be of the highest class known, to avoid enthusiastic rushes with their pens, and to seat themselves at their desks day by day as though they were lawyer's clerks;—and so let them sit until the allotted task shall be accomplished.

Developing a Writer's Attitude

With athletes, with lovers, with writers, attitude predicts performance. When I first taught news writing I did not know if it could be taught. I came from the professional world of journalism and I realized that even if I drove my students hard, I could not assign in a semester the amount of reporting and writing they would do in a week in a city room.

Yet the students who took my course—and the editors who hired them—reported that they did well. I investigated and discovered that I had unknowingly taught—and modeled—the city-room attitude. I had consciously taught the techniques of writing news, but what they had learned were the attitudes I unconsciously modeled. They could find fragmentary and contradictory information about an event, confirm its accuracy, order the fragments into meaning and share that meaning in a terse, clear and graceful style—all within ridiculous limits of time and space. My students were not surprised by the demands of the daily newspaper, radio or television news room. They were ready to learn their craft.

The longer I taught other courses and observed my own learning, the more I realized the importance of "attitude predicts performance." If my students expected to fail, they failed; if I expected to write badly, I wrote badly. The product produced was as much the result of attitude as it was of skill. The four attitudes that are most important to this publishing writer are:

Your Difference Is Your Strength

It took me about sixty-eight of my seventy-one years to understand this. The understanding came when I read some comments on writing by Sandra Cisneros who said, "Imagine yourself at your kitchen table, in your pajamas. Imagine one person you'd allow to see you that way, and write in the voice you'd use to that friend." That's excellent advice—put it over your writing desk—but then, in the same paragraph, came the insight that so affected me: "Write about what makes you different."

I felt a great weight lift from me. Of course I had been writing about what made me different but I had felt guilty about it. The struggle to be myself was hard as e. e. cummings said, "To be nobody-but-yourself—in a world which is doing its best, night and day, to make you everybody else—means to fight the hardest battle which any human being can fight; and never stop fighting."

All the qualities that made me weird in my family, in school, on the street corner, in the Army, on the newspaper or magazine staff and as a member of a university faculty, the qualities I usually tried to hide and was often ashamed of, were what made me the writer I am.

Some of the qualities that made me different from the people around me were my ability to be deeply involved and distantly detached simultaneously, living my life and observing it; my curiosity about others—call it gossip; my need to shape experience into story, finding meaning in confusion; my feeling that reflection—remembered and reshaped experience—provides the true reality; my delight in word play; my obsessive need to share what I see, think, feel; my attraction to those human activities, emotions, thoughts that are not supposed to be discussed. These qualities may make me a discomforting friend or an embarrassing relative, but they also make me a writer. As writers, we should accept and develop our own individual, even eccentric, response to the world.

And ironically, the more personal, the more individual you become, the more universally you will be read. As Sara Paretsky says, "The more you withdraw inside yourself, the more honest you are. The more willing you are to sort of cut yourself all the way down to the bone, the more common you will make your experience. The more public you are, the more you lose that focus."

Respect Your Draft

Watch a cabinet maker at work and you will see respect for the wood; watch Minnie Mae make bread and you will see her respect for the grains that make up the dough. Soon after we met, she talked of respect being as important as love in a relationship. Respect is, in fact, the highest order of love.

If you could watch an effective writer at work, you would observe the respect a writer has for each draft. Writing becomes a matter of collaboration, the writer following the draft, the writer receiving instruction from the draft, the writer nurturing the draft, the writer serving as midwife to meaning.

Picasso made many statements that revealed his loving respect for his work:

> To know what you want to draw, you have to begin drawing. If it turns out to be a man, I draw a man. If it turns out to be a woman, I draw a woman.
>
> * * *
>
> A picture is not thought out and settled beforehand. While it is being done it changes as one's thoughts change. And when it is finished, it still goes on changing, according to the state of mind of whoever is looking at it.
>
> * * *
>
> Painting is stronger than I am. It makes me do what it wants.

It took me a long time to learn to respect my drafts. I did not realize that my failures were instructive. As experimental failures instruct the scientist so do experiments in meaning and speaking instruct the writer, what can't be done revealing what may be done.

I have to accept—even encourage—a kind of essential dumbness in the face of writing. I remember some of our college hockey players at dinner at our house, telling their All-American goalie not to think. They were kidding the goalie but, as is often the case, there was truth in the teasing. The goalie has to respond to the play as it develops. If the goalie thinks—goes through an intellectual process of analyzing the shot and considering alternatives—the puck will be in the net before the goalie acts. I think the writer is often in that situation. As writers we need to study our craft, our language, our rhetoric, our literature, but at the moment of writing we have to be instinctive. We can think too much about what we may write, plan too carefully, force a draft toward intention while the effective draft qualifies, limits, focuses, even contradicts intention.

Writers must learn to have faith in the writing act; they are led by the writing to discover what they have to say and how it may be said. Of course, there is training, education, practice, plan, experience. Intuition is absorbed tradition, but at the moment of writing the act is more like jazz improvisation than bricklaying.

It is the writer's job to help the meaning free itself as it is the sculptor's job to free the lion that lies waiting in the block of marble.

Talent Is Common; Energy Rare

Looking back at my classmates who wanted to write; the soldiers I served with who wanted to become writers after the war; the secret writers of novels, poems, and plays who sat near me in the city room; the faculty members who imagined writing great books; my students who wanted to become published writers; I realize the difference between the few who became writers and the many who did not was not talent but energy.

Talent is cheap. I have always been surrounded by colleagues, friends, students who were more talented than I am. In fact, when I wrote with elementary-school students, I was always at about the middle of the class. My wife has a great deal of talent and she has published three of the four pieces she has written, but whole decades have gone by when she has not needed to write.

The rarity is the person who places the rear end in the chair at the writing desk, day after day. I don't worry about talent. Most have more talent than I, but they will not write. They cannot overcome their fear, they do not need to write, or they have not learned the writer's secret that writing produces energy. It is the writing—the excitement of discovering what I didn't know I knew, the delight of craft, the satisfaction of sharing—that gives me the energy to write.

Acceptance Is as Irrational as Rejection

That is the advice I give all who ask me how to become writers. I had a novel rejected because it was the story of a quadriplegic, and most of it took place in hospitals. The editor described a Marlon Brando movie, *The Men*, in talking about my book. Clearly he hadn't read it, but just as clearly he had a psychological terror of illness and hospitals. Within hours the same manuscript, without a single change, was accepted by another editor who, it turns out, was a hypochondriac. His hobby was being sick. He loved the book.

We all tend to believe that acceptance is rational, an example of literary standards at work. The danger in that is that we may find lessons from one acceptance that are not universally true. We can all extrapolate many lessons from acceptance, but you may have been accepted because the editor has a one-thousand-word hole and no essays that length, because he or she needs a piece by a woman or a man, because he or she wants a piece on rape or gardening.

You cannot second guess what goes on in the editorial mind—or the editorial meeting. On top of that, editorial policies—and editors—are constantly changing.

The solution is to write what you have to write.

Rejection is easier to protect yourself against than acceptance, but again, you have no more understanding of why an editor rejects a piece than you have when someone refuses a date with you. It may be because you dress too formally, because the person is on a diet, or because the person is already involved with somebody else. People rarely offer their real reasons for rejection; often they do not know the real reasons. "This person is not for me"; "this manuscript is not for us." There is as much literary reason as there is reason that ties are wide or thin, skirts long or short.

Professional writers are often assigned projects where the instruction is clear and we deliver to command, but our best writing comes from our own instruction.

Since we live in an irrational world of publication, we cannot market our speculative writing, calculating what will sell, we can best do the writing we need to do, the writing we must do, and do it our own way, giving individual voice to individual experience.

2

Starting to Write

Write What?

Where do you get your ideas?

I don't have ideas. If I had ideas I would be a philosopher or theologian, historian or political scientist, not a writer.

I try to imagine what it would be like to be swollen with ideas: a large head, thick glasses, Oxford stoop, seated on a tall stool before great leather books, inscribing an idea on parchment with a quill pen.

Beginning writers make the mistake of looking for ideas before beginning to write. They must welcome the hint, the clue, become suspicious of developed ideas, even fear the idea that is so complete—so authoritative—it does not allow surprise. When someone offers me a developed idea for a column, an article, or a book, my defenses mobilize even if the person is an editor. Ideas—theories, concepts—are seductive. They sum up, explain, clarify, define, limit; the idea-giver has done the writer's work.

Ideas are finished, but my shop is designed to process unfinished work that will continue to change in the minds of my readers. I am not going to try to tell them what to think but to stimulate their own thinking. When I write well, we think together, examining our shared world until we must go our separate ways, seeing our individual landscapes and drawing our individual maps to reveal the meaning of experience.

Ideas hunger for consistency. They become theories and bodies of thought, systems, ologies. The writer must practice inconsistency, building up the tower of blocks and then knocking it down. The writer's creation comes as much from destruction as construction. The writer fights his or her own civil war, always remaining an enemy to the writer's own written texts: what is done must be undone.

Ideas often control the conclusion of a piece of writing. It is dangerous for the writer to know exactly where he or she is going. The writer works best by serendipity and accident, catching the vision out of the corner of the eye. The writer's material is what is half-overheard, not quite understood, what disappears around a corner before it can be studied.

Receptivity

The writer has to achieve a passive alertness—perhaps the hunter waiting in the duck blind, perhaps the lover waiting for a marriage proposal, perhaps the state trooper hidden just over the rise in the turnpike. The writer has to become receptive, open to gesture, to a slight adjustment in a tone of voice, to what is different from yesterday, to what will be different tomorrow, to fleeting thoughts and changes in feelings as subtle as an offshore breeze that hints of rain.

Robert Frost talked of writing topics being like burrs that stick to you when you walk through a field. Denise Levertov says, "It is a sort of vague feeling that somewhere in the vicinity there is a poem . . . You can smell the poem before you can see it. Like some animal." E. B. White explains, "When a mosquito bites me—I scratch. When I write something, I guess I'm trying to get rid of the itchiness inside me."

The itch is what keeps coming to mind; what you think about when you are not thinking; when you are walking, jogging, driving, shopping, waiting for someone; what comes to mind as you go to bed or when you wake in the night; what you find yourself talking about, worrying about, scratching in your memory or your imagination.

Tune in the blankness. When students complained that they felt empty when they sat down to write, I congratulated them. Writing often begins in darkness and despair, in hopelessness and need. Accept this emptiness. Go further. Tune into the blankness and the state of emptiness does not remain. Images. Words. Phrases. Scenes. Faces. Each passes through the darkness like shooting stars.

Then one reappears. Once. Again. A third time. Perhaps it collides with another star. Perhaps it only passes close by. Perhaps a third appears and disappears.

You have something to write about.

Let me try it. I descend to panic, ignoring all the topics that I have noted in my daybook or in my head. I ignore the subjects that have ripened as I have talked to myself. I force myself to where I have nothing to say. I decide I will think about the silence in my family when I was young, the way we hurt each other by turning away.

> summer evening at home . . . high school . . . Chester street . . . upstairs flat . . . brown . . . dark brown woodwork . . . brown wicker furniture . . . father's brown oak desk . . . brown china cabinet . . . brown wallpaper . . . brown people . . . brown food . . . brown floors and rugs . . . brown clothes . . . brown—sepia—photo of grandfather—brown engravings from a better time before I was born . . . brown frames around mirror . . . how I spied by watching mirrors . . . reflections in glass covering steel engravings . . . watching.

There is nothing here about silence but that's the way the writer's mind works. It follows its own need—and the wise writer trots along. Once I had written the lines above, I kept seeing Grandma, Mother, Father, myself reflected in the mirror of memory and the next morning I found myself writing:

NIGHT WATCH

From her bed Grandma could turn
her hand mirror to watch us
in the living room or twist it
to see who closed the bathroom door.

I stood on the back porch, watched
Mother in the mirror over the bedroom
dresser as she stood in the kitchen
kneading, kneading Wednesday meat loaf.

After our silent supper, I stayed
at the table, saw in black night windows,
Father turn from Mother, Mother
turn from him, re-enter her romance.

I crept to the hall where Mother's
shadow stretched from her reading lamp,
stepped on the shadow with all my weight,
saw her watching me, saw her smile.

In the china cabinet door, I saw Father,
his rimless glasses reflecting me, nod,
turn away from me, from Mother, then
turn back, watching us from the door.

In the framed etching of Tobermoray
I caught the glint of Grandma's mirror
as she watched Father watching
Mother watching me.

Tonight I turn quickly, just in time
to catch, in the night black glass
of the patio door, Grandma standing,
Mother, Father, younger than I am now.

I am frightened by the poem, especially the violence of my stepping on her shadow. I have no specific memory of this incident, but it is true now that I have written it and it is all too true in the violence of Mother's smile and Father's reaction to my act. Those few lines have caught an entire way of life and somehow, in capturing it, I can study it and begin to live with it, to understand why it was that way and how I am influenced by it so many years later.

Most writers do not have many fields to plow. My writing mostly comes from my going over—and over and over again—a few territories: my peculiar childhood with an invalid grandmother, my fascination with the writing process, failure in school, the war; that's about it.

The following poem, cousin to the one above, did not begin as an idea about war or the way boys are prepared for war but as an image of myself sitting on the rug playing with lead toy soldiers. I didn't know what the image meant but it itched, there seemed to be something significant about it. I had to write to find out what the significance was. In the poem I encountered the violence that becomes a young boy's preparation for combat.

BEFORE THE WAR

We keep an eye
on Grandma
in the glass
that protects
the steel engraving
of Tobermoray
in spring

her invalid bed
her gaping mouth
the covers' slow rise
and fall

she keeps her eye
on us

Edith's husband plays
Depression Solitaire
with sales tags
from the store

Edith lives
a better life
in her woman's
magazine

the boy
lines up
lead soldiers
knocks them down

My emptiness gave me a subject. The emptiness was insulation against the busyness of life, the news and the gossip that clutter my day, the command of the "to do" list. Accept your own emptiness and the well may fill.

As you develop the habit of looking inside yourself you will find that you become more aware of the world around you. Internal and external awareness interact. My poem might have come from an external stimulus.

At Thanksgiving I glance in the dining room mirror, catch a grandson at play in the living room, and think:

> josh is in the mirror . . . plays with a plastic space ship . . . my dump truck . . . my lead soldiers . . . British Army . . . great fur hats . . . red coats . . . my great uncle fought Napoleon in the Battle of Waterloo . . . named for him . . . when I went overseas Grandma thought I was going to Waterloo . . . heard war stories when she was a girl . . . Dad wants me to have his war . . . he missed his . . . hope josh doesn't have his war . . . brought up in a house of peace and love . . . still at three plays war games . . . "I hero. I Batman." . . . play school, sure, but . . . is it bred into him . . . he looks up . . . catches me watching him in the mirror . . . smiles . . . doesn't know I'm watching myself play with soldiers . . . playing soldier not so many years later . . . how we lived before my war

From such moments of reverie and reflection can come an essay, articles, books, plays, poems, short stories, columns.

When people ask me when I knew I was a writer, I answer that I was a writer long before I knew there were writers. My becoming a writer was born out of an awareness that, in turn, was born out of loneliness that contained a need to observe carefully to understand and a need to escape.

I was born into a world I could not understand, as we all are. I had to try and make sense of the contradictions of my daily life. The Bible and my parents said to honor my father and my mother, but each of my parents told me how dreadful the other person was. My parents said "love thy neighbor" but they hated, feared, and felt superior to our Irish Catholic neighbors. Jesus threw the money changers out of the temple but my father hungered for the financial success that would give him status in Tremont Temple Baptist Church. I made up stories that failed to make sense of my world but I would catch glimpses of order and tell myself other stories that might bring at least momentary meaning to confusion (to paraphrase Robert Frost).

And I made up stories to escape. My real family—the one I felt I belonged to—lived in the wall. In my stories I hit the home run, the most beautiful girl in the class asked me to take her to the movies, and I became a hero in the war that was just over the horizon. Day dream and night dream blurred, so that even today I am never quite sure what I have lived and what I have made believe.

I suspect that you have been as aware of your life as I have, perhaps more so, but you may not have admitted it until the page revealed the life you have lived. Making out in the back seat, lost in the throes of teenage passion, your eyes were wide open watching what was going on in the front seat; or perhaps you left your body and looked back down, recording with a disturbing clinical detachment what was happening to your "other" you. When you observe and connect, you are writing. When Ernest Hemingway was asked where he worked, he allegedly answered, "In my head."

Write a discovery draft. Often I don't know what has been written in my head so I write a discovery draft. This is frequently called free writing, but I don't like that term because you quickly learn that it isn't free, that the text makes connections, reveals a pattern, establishes a trail toward meaning. You discover what you have to say by letting go of preconceptions, by resisting intent.

In writing a discovery draft, I type as fast as I can, sometimes with the computer screen turned off. The important thing is to hear the flow of text. The pace, intensity, and music of the draft often reveals the feelings and the thoughts that produce an effective writing idea. I hear something that surprises me and I must pursue it.

Focus on an itch. As we work toward our subject, we concentrate on E. B. White's itch; our language keeps returning to the same place the way the tongue seeks a cavity in a tooth. Many times the subject is something we resist exploring—the fact I was in the other room when they removed extraordinary means from my daughter, Lee, and she died, the fact that I was capable of killing in war, the fact that I have not yet come to the compassion for my mother I seek—but then I remember Donald Barthelme's advice, "Write about what you're most afraid of."

When I do that it is always a healing activity and when I publish my writing, reader response tells me I have articulated the unspoken feelings and thoughts of many readers.

What Does a Subject Look Like?

After years of lying in wait for a subject to explore in writing I have begun to develop a personal field guide for the hunter-writer. In small fragments I find the greatest possibilities.

Line. Most of my writing begins with a line, a fragment of language—a word, a clause, sometimes a sentence—that contains a tension that will ignite writing. I have been working on a book for years that grew out of the line in my daybook that I had "an ordinary war." And I did. I was not killed or wounded; I did not suffer combat fatigue, at least not enough to be treated for it; I was neither awarded a medal nor charged with cowardice; but, having said that, I started remembering what becomes ordinary in infantry combat and I have a mystery I must explore by writing.

When a line occurs to me—*sees self in window black with night, feels the weight of August sun on his arm, return of no-neck football players means end of summer, father and I got along better on long distance calls*—I write it down in my daybook or on one of the 3" x 5" cards I carry in a shirt pocket. I don't know what each line means and that's what attracts me, that's what itches. When I release the tension within it, I will have a draft.

Image. Other times writing will start with a mental picture. I live in a visual world, as do most writers. With a different teacher I might have become an artist and that is true of many of the writers I know. I sketch in a sketchbook that is always near me; I sketch in my mind, recording what I see—and editing it so it reveals more than what I have seen. When I write I am often just recording in words what I see or what I remember with my mind's eye. In this seeing with language, however, I realize that my brain has recorded more than what I was aware of at the time of actual seeing.

I may see someone turn away, and in writing a story about it I may discover that cold anger is worse than rage, that not doing can inflict more pain that a fist. Our visions are different and, as we have said before, we should pay attention to our difference. Spring is a joyous time for most people, and it is for me, but I was aware one day of an unexpected sadness, almost a fear of spring. The gentle image of the spring landscape behind my house was so discomforting I had to write to understand it or, at least, to put it to rest.

APRIL HARVEST

A tiny patch of fur
revealed by the retreat of snow,
brown, almost black, something once living.

Another April, in Germany, at the end of war,
I stood sentinel as winter soldiers rose through snow melt,
bloated, bursting from uniforms that made one friend,
one foe.

An unexploded bomb, the bones of the cow
mistaken for a tank, a boot, a foot, a hand reaching
up from earth, a mess kit with half a pork chop,
potato, peas, a snapped off bayonet, a blossom
of browned bandage, a ring of morphine needles, used,
a skull with three eyes, a snapshot: two blond boys,
a woman in a bathing suit, a letter with purple ink
run into dancing squiggles that might be German,
might be English, a clavicle, a shin bone
no longer attached to the knee bone, a line of mines
waiting for that final stumbling, stupid step,
the god damned yellow green of tree bud, plant shoot,
spring grass, weed, bush, leaf, vine, that will grow over history,
invite tourists to walk our battlefield,
maps in hand, ears wired to audio guides, smiling
at talk of fallen heroes who gave their lives
for a fucking flag.

I leave my woods, sick from the sweet stink of Spring,
the dank dark sucking muck, slick slime of autumn leaves,
log rot, the stiff flat garter snake, smeared smudge
of feathers that once were crow or hawk and flew,
the patch of fur,
April harvest.

Note that the last line—"April harvest"—had the tension within it that could have made it an instigating line. It has within it the conflict that could have begun the poem.

Specific. Subjects for writing also come from a resonating specific, a detail that sparks implications:

- Death and injury in infantry combat often comes from flying body parts.
- I was plugged into a heart-lung machine for 91 minutes.
- I was so short I had to take two reefs in my apron when I first started working in a meat market.
- In my home all disease could be cured with a glass of Cliquot Club Golden Ginger Ale.
- My father's mother and father indentured themselves as factory workers to come to this country.
- A baseball catcher has to throw to a second base he cannot see when he is in his crouch.

The world is full of details that can ignite writing. Look, listen, record, play with them in your mind and on paper. Specifics are attracted to other specifics. That Cliquot Club Golden Ginger Ale led to slimy boiled spinach to greasy beef fat to smooth chicken fat to grainy bacon fat and I had a column on the "health foods" of my childhood.

Question. Subjects come as questions and develop as questions. Why do doctors use the term *procedure*? Why do corporations use the terms *outplacement* and *downsizing* instead of *firing* and *cutting out jobs*? Why did our government talk of *body count* during the Vietnam War? What is the danger to us of using this sort of language? Why is it important to translate? How do we teach our students to read the true meaning of such terms? Now, there's a subject if you update it with this year's jargon.

Problem. A squirrel faced with a bird-feeder baffle and a writer seeking a subject are both problem-solving animals. The problem may involve subject matter. How do we motivate students who have no mentors or models in their home or neighborhood who know how society works? How do we convince taxpayers that schools are a good investment? That's obvious, isn't it? Well, why isn't it to some people, and what might convince them?

The problem may lie within the draft. How do we write as a child? How do we reveal the harm done in a home in which there are no fights because everyone turns away from each other, hurts by silence? How do we write with emotion without being emotional? How do we show what characters are thinking by the way they speak?

But I've been assigned a subject. As we begin to get published, editors may ask for pieces of writing. I often get requests for pieces from the point of view of an old timer or a veteran. I just did a piece on our dropping the atomic bomb on Hiroshima and Nagasaki from the point of view of someone who was in the service at the time. The challenge when you have been assigned a subject is to make it yours.

I listen to what the editor has to say about the purpose of the piece, how it fits into a special issue, the length, the deadline, but I pay little attention to what the editor says about the subject. That is my job. I will make it mine and I set the deadline ahead so if the editor doesn't like what I write, I can do revision or someone else can be assigned to the subject.

I go into the subject, allowing my mind to circle the territory like a dog sniffing around a new back yard. I may write a list of specifics looking for specifics or a line or an image that surprises me. I look for what I do not expect, what contradicts, confuses, complicates, connects, discomforts and then I write a discovery draft as fast as I can to race ahead of preconception.

If I am going to write about ethics, I have to find personal examples that engage me with the topic: the red rubber ball I shoplifted from Woolworth's, how I felt when my mother made me lie to the landlord, the way in which I betrayed a friend's confidence. The writing does not have to be personal in tone or subject, but the writer's engagement with the topic should be. The research may be in the library and the tone scholarly, but the motivation to explore this subject usually comes from the writer's personal need to explore the subject.

Write what you need to write. Write to explore what you don't know and want to know. Write about what makes you laugh or cry, angry or happy, surprised or puzzled, worried or satisfied. And if none of that works, just write. The draft will tell you what you are interested in, what bugs you, what itches, what you need to know. Writing will reveal your subject.

Listening to Your Voice

The most important element in writing is the music of meaning we call voice. I am always impressed by how quickly our best writers established both their own individual voices and the voice of a particular piece of writing. Read these examples of voice and you will hear them rise off the page. To emphasize that heard quality, read them aloud.

Dorothy Allison, in her autobiographical *Bastard Out of Carolina*:

> I've been called Bone all my life, but my name's Ruth Anne. I was named for and by my oldest aunt—Aunt Ruth. My mama didn't have much to say about it, since strictly speaking, she wasn't there.

Allison establishes her separateness—and loneness—right away, the distance she feels from those about her, and her challenging, non self-pitying tough voice reveals how she will look at her life—with wit, anger, compassion, humor, but never self-pity.

Joseph Mitchell, "Old Mr. Flood," from *Up in the Old Hotel*:

> [Mr. Flood] eats with relish every kind of seafood, including sea-urchin eggs, blowfish tails, svinkles, ink squids, and barn-door skates. He especially likes an ancient Boston breakfast dish—fried cod tongues, cheeks, and sounds, sounds being the gelatinous air bladders along the cod's backbone.

Mitchell's voice relishes the specific and the strange and the reader knows the writer will take him into a familiar world that will quickly become unfamiliar, that reader and writer will delight in the unexpected, what is different, eccentric, interesting.

Howard Norman, *The Northern Lights*:

> My father brought home a radio. "It's got a sender and a receiver," he said. "Now you can talk to people other than yourselves." He fit the earphones over my head. And the first news I heard was that my friend Pelly Bay had drowned. Pelly had fallen through the ice while riding his unicycle. That was April 1959.

Norman uses a deceptively simple voice to get inside the head of a boy whose world immediately enlarges and comes close. He—and the reader—will never be quite the same after these 59 words.

Zora Neale Hurston, *Dust Tracks on a Road*:

> So the old man died in high favor with everybody. He had done his cussing and fighting and drinking as became a man, taken care of his family and accumulated property. Nobody thought anything about his going to the county seat frequently, getting drunk, getting his riding-mule drunk along with him, and coming down the pike yelling and singing while his mule brayed in drunken hilarity. There went a man.

Hurston, in her conversational voice, has established a world and a view of the world that is not distant and critical but intimate and understanding.

What Is Voice?

Voice is the music of your language, the music of your meaning. Writers use the term *voice* rather than the term *style* for several reasons. The word *style* implies that you can buy it off the rack, but the term *voice* implies that it is personal. Voice can be tuned to different purposes, be detached or institutional, but it begins with the individual voice. Voice also emphasizes the heard quality of written language. Voice is what we hear the individual writer—the text—saying.

The Importance of Voice

Voice is the single most important element in attracting and holding a reader's interest. We know it is the voice of Beethoven or Mozart, Nirvana or R.E.M., that compels us to listen, but we do not always realize it is the voice that draws us to an author. If we examine the columnists, novelists, playwrights, poets, political commentators, textbook writers we read, we find that it is voice that makes us return to those pages or pick up a new text.

But voice is not only significant after publication; it serves the writer in the earliest stages of writing. E. L. Doctorow says, " . . . it wasn't until I was able to find the voice and forget about the intention that I was able to write the book." Eudora Welty explains the importance of voice to her: "It is to me the voice of the story or the poem itself. The cadence, whatever it is that asks you to believe, the feeling that resides in the printed word, reaches me through the reader-voice . . . When I write and the sound of it comes back to my ears, then I act to make my changes. I have always trusted this voice."

Writers discover their emotional relationship to a subject through voice. Even thinking about the subject before taking notes, or in making notes, or in drafting they hear the concern, laughter, anger, sadness, happiness that reveals how they feel about the subject. In the same way, writers discover what they think about the subject and even what it means as they hear the voice of the draft. The movie soundtrack often announces the villain, predicts the attack, celebrates the resolution. Written language—as it is being written—has a soundtrack the experienced writer can hear.

Tess Gallagher explains, "The sound often precedes the meaning, the sound of what the experience is . . . Music comes first. If you get the music right, the meaning often follows or begins to evolve. Meaning doesn't precede music. And what I'm doing in the drafting is trying to get the music and the meaning to come together."

Establishing trust is also vital in writing, and voice convinces the writer looking for a subject and the reader looking for a writer. Readers are attracted to a writer because they believe the author's voice and are moved, entertained, persuaded by it. The sound of the text supports and, sometimes, even reveals the meaning of the text to the reader.

What Are the Elements of Voice?

Voice is one of the most complex and yet least-investigated areas of composition. It is a subject that often makes academics uncomfortable because it does not seem intellectual, but we all speak and write with voice. The absence of voice—the personal in writing—is also a voice, the voice of detachment and disinterest that may be appropriate depending on the subject and what the writer needs to say about it.

Let's take an example and reveal common elements of voice. I've chosen Alice Munro because her voice is so powerful and yet so plain—ordinary words used in unusual combinations so they reveal truths that we immediately recognize, and knowledge we didn't know we had until Munro spoke it for us. In her short story, "Five Points," Munro takes only a few lines to reveal a relationship to establish, through voice, an attitude towards the relationship that is critcal, compassionate, humorous, empathetic and sad.

> They have a history of passion, the way families have a history, or people who have gone to school together. They don't have much else. They've never eaten a meal with each other, or seen a movie. But they've come through some complicated adventures together, and dangers—not just of the stopping-on-the-highway kind. They've taken risks, surprising each other, always correctly. In dreams you can have the feeling that you've had this dream before, that you have this dream over and over again, and you know that it's really nothing that simple. You know that there's a whole underground system that you call "dreams," having nothing better to call them, and that this system is not like roads or tunnels but more like a live body network, all coiling and stretching, unpredictable but finally familiar—where you are now, where you've always been. That was the way it was with them and sex, going somewhere like that, and they understood the same things about it and trusted each other, so far.

Revealing specifics. "They've never eaten a meal with each other, or seen a movie." Voice, like all good writing, is built on the delivery of significant information to the reader.

The word. "History" not "a record of," "passion" not "love." Note how her simple words are right—they reveal meaning.

The phrase. The phrase is often overlooked in studying writing, but the text often takes off from the igniting phrase. In the phrase, two or three common words spark a new meaning when they touch each other. "History of passion" both expands and contracts the relationship.

The beat. Voice has rhythm, a pattern of beats and pauses that support meaning. Read this paragraph aloud noticing its pacing, the way it slows down, speeds up, and, for a fine example of the beat at the end: comma—pause—"so far."

The point of view. Voice reveals the writer, the character of the writer, the way the writer views the world. Notice the distance at which Alice Munro stands from the subject. She is close enough to know and reveal the characters' intimate life, distanced enough to put it in context; close enough to care but not judge, distant enough to see and reveal what is destined to happen. She has compassion, wisdom, and humor as she tells this story.

The Personal Voice

Our writing voices—we have not one but many, like our speaking voices—are at first personal and individual. They are composed of many forces:

- Our family, genetic background. We can tell which member of the family is speaking from the other room.
- Our ethnic heritage. When I visit Scotland, I can understand a Scots burr so thick the rest of my family thinks the native is speaking Gaelic.
- Our childhood neighborhoods. Sometimes I laugh when my friend Kell speaks. We were brought up in similar south-of-Boston communities and have traces of that dialect in our speech.
- Our present neighborhoods. My New Hampshire daughter has lived in New York since she graduated from college and her voice—written and spoken—is beginning to reveal it.
- Our roles in life. I speak City Room and Army and Football and Police and University and English Department and Professor and Cardiac Patient and Father and Husband and Grandfather and Close Friend and Neighbor and Acquaintance. In this book, I write with a fellow writer's voice and, at times, with the voice of a fellow teacher.

Our voices have these elements and more. When I am speaking I sometimes hear traces of the evangelist that I have not been for fifty years. The voice on which we build is personal and is ever changing as our experiences at living change.

The trick is to accept your own voice, not to imitate a "literary" voice, the voice of a writer you admire, but to accept the individual qualities of your natural voice—the voice that marks you as different, the voice that reveals your character, your vision of the world—and to strengthen it so that you can write with increased effectiveness.

The Voice of the Text

During the 1970s there was a cult of the present voice in composition teaching. It was called the "authentic voice" and it was considered important for teachers to recognize the individual voice because historically, schools had emphasized a detached, mass, academic voice that denied the rich differences between us. But, like many good ideas, it went too far and seemed to allow people to write in a self-indulgent manner: "Hey, like awful, I mean I never knew death could be so, like, gross."

The effective writer tunes the individual voice to the purpose and meaning of the text as well as to the reader. This does not mean the writer abandons the natural voice, but instead tunes it to the writing. We all speak somewhat differently when we visit a hospital room, when we are in church, when we are on the playing field, when we are called to the boss's office, when we teach, when we are being taught. Each hour we tune our personal, individual voices to the task at hand.

Let's go back to Alice Munro. If she were writing a marriage counselor's report she might say, "The wife had a long-term extramarital relationship that seemed limited to sexual activity" rather than, "They have a history of passion."

Writing Your Voice

To discover your voice, write fast and write out loud. Velocity will drive you into naturalness and allow you to outrun the censors—teachers, classmates, colleagues—that inhibit you and make you want to write in someone else's voice. You will begin to sound like yourself.

And you need to hear your words before you see them on the screen or the page. If you work on a word processor, turn off the monitor. You should find it no great loss during the writing of a first draft. Effective writers hear what they are saying as they say it and actually pace and tune their sentences between the moment they are heard and the words appear on the screen.

Tuning Your Voice

The writer tunes the individual voice so that it serves the need of the text. Listen to E. Annie Proulx, a wonderfully skilled writer with an exceptionally strong voice, plunge you right into her novel *Postcards* in just a few lines. Read the following paragraphs aloud.

> Even before he got up he knew he was on his way. Even in the midst of the involuntary orgasmic jerking he knew. Knew she was dead, knew he was on his way. Even standing there on shaking legs, trying to push the copper buttons through the stiff buttonholes he knew that everything he had done or thought in his life had to be started over again. Even if he got away.

> He couldn't get any air, but stood on his knocked-out legs gasping and wheezing. It was like he'd taken a bad fall. Dazed. He could feel the blood hammering in his throat. But there was nothing else, only the gasping for breath and an abnormal acuity of vision. Mats of juniper flowed across the field like spilled water; doghair maple crowded the stone wall wavering through the trees.
>
> He'd thought of the wall walking up the slope behind Billy, thought of it in a common way, of working on it sometime, setting back in place the stones that frost and thrusting roots had thrown out. Now he saw it as a scene drawn in powerful ink lines, the rock fissured with crumpled strings of quartz, humps of moss like shoulders shrugging out of the mold, black lignum beneath rotten bark, the aluminum sheen of deadwood.
>
> A stone the size and shape of a car's backseat jutted out of the wall, and below it was a knob of soil that marked the entrance to an abandoned fox den. Oh Jesus, it wasn't his fault but they'd say it was. He grasped Billy's ankles and dragged her to the wall. He rolled her up under the stone, could not look at her face. There was already a waxiness to her body. The texture of her bunched stockings, the shape of her nails glowed with the luminous hardness that marks the newly dead in the moment before the flames consume or the sucking water pulls them under. The space beneath the rock was shallow. Her arm fell outward, the hand relaxed, the fingers curled as if she held a hand mirror or a Fourth of July flag.

Proulx places us in the main character's head and we share with him that extraordinary attention to detail that comes in a traumatic moment. We also know that the character has taken an irreversible step and, by reading the novel, we will find out how his life has changed and what it means.

The voice of the novel communicates the character's emotional state and also the flowing river of events. Proulx has said this book was "a road book and because Loyal was a character who wandered at random, I wanted that spacy, random, stumbled-across, maybe-it-happened-maybe-it-didn't feeling in it." The music of the novel supports that feeling.

Now read—aloud—the beginning of another novel of hers that has an equally strong but a very different, abrupt voice that is appropriate for this novel.

> Here is an account of a few years in the life of Quoyle, born in Brooklyn and raised in a shuffle of dreary upstate towns.
>
> Hive-spangled, gut roaring with gas and cramp, he survived childhood; at the state university, hand clapped over his chin, he camouflaged torment

> with smiles and silence. Stumbled through his twenties and into his thirties learning to separate his feelings from his life, counting on nothing. He ate prodigiously, liked a ham knuckle, buttered spuds.
>
> His jobs: distributor of vending machine candy, all-night clerk in a convenience store, a third-rate newspaperman. At thirty-six, bereft, brimming with grief and thwarted love, Quoyle steered away to Newfoundland, the rock that had generated his ancestors, a place he had never been nor thought to go.

The author explained the voice of this novel, which won the Pulitzer prize: "You may have seen the old newspapers that used to have a lot of subheads. Each story had these subheads that were just tiny, compressed *precis* of what the story was about, one after another. I thought if I cast my sentences in 'subheadese' it would give a newspapery flavor to the whole book. So that's what I had in mind when I went to that very terse, truncated kind of style. But it didn't work that way."

I think it did. The newspaper novel does capture the quick, immediate quality of news writing; but the writer goes on, "How it worked was an internalization of Quoyle's thoughts and actions. So it *did* work, but not quite as I had intended. I'm not displeased with it because we often talk that way, in bits and pieces and chunks of sentences, with much left out. So it had a flavor of conversation or immediacy to it, too, which was okay for that particular story."

She continues talking about voice, calling it style: "The style and sentence structure, the rhythm, the balance—all these things I take a lot of trouble with—must suit the story. To find a style that's just right for the story you're doing takes some experimentation and fooling around. I did try writing *The Shipping News*, a chapter or two, with longer sentences and just didn't like it as much. It was tiresome."

We all have many voices. We are used to tuning our voices to the sick room, to the love room, to the office, to the store, to the auto accident. In writing, we tune the voice, as Proulx does, to the purpose of the text. The result is the voice of the text that has distanced itself from us and becomes its own person as our children do after they leave home.

To allow the voice its chance to develop we have to listen as we write and encourage those words, phrases, lines, those rhythms and pauses, that clarify the text. We are led, in writing, by the sound of the evolving draft. It is our job to listen and respect the voice of the draft, the most important element in nurturing a draft that will be heard by readers.

Inviting Surprise

When I sit at my writing desk to begin a new column, poem or book, I often think of the question that Graham Greene asked, "Isn't disloyalty as much the writer's virtue as loyalty is the soldier's?"

Yes. Writers should stand at the edge of the community: close enough for compassion, distant enough to be critical. Writers must not only be disloyal to others but, most of all, disloyal to themselves, to their own beliefs, their own vision of the world. I feel no need to be consistent; what I have written before should not predict or control what I may write today. I come to my writing desk as innocent as possible of what I have already published.

I write to discover what I am thinking, not what I have already thought. And I return—obsessively—to the few subjects I need to explore—and re-explore—in writing. I must write and in the writing process, attempt to understand my childhood, to come to terms with what I was able to do as a soldier in World War II, to confront illness and death. I try to write about other subjects, but when my writing goes well I find myself drawn back to one of those four personal territories. I write not to confirm or document what I know about them but to discover what I do not yet know. If I am to surprise myself with fresh insight, I need to be disloyal to what I have written—thought, felt, believed, remembered—before.

I was surprised and honored when Dr. Donna Qualley, in her dissertation completed at the University of New Hampshire in 1994—*Writing and Reading as Reflexive Inquiry*—described my disloyalty:

> Over the years, Murray has shown me the importance of the provisional, the tentative, or what I have come to think of as 'the learner's stance,' a stance that names itself in the here and now, that can explain how it came to be, but that remains open to the possibility of further complication and change. I find that I am more likely to trust those people who adopt such an approach toward their work because this mind-set always seems to me the most rational (and most ethical) way to be.

Even when I do a new edition of a textbook, I chart the new chapters and sections from memory, often even writing them before I fit them into the parts of the previous edition that will be saved. When I return to my novel, I do not read what I have written before. My poems are written as if I had never written a poem on the subject before. My articles—and talks—on writing and teaching writing are begun with the conscious act of forgetting what I have said—and believed—before. If I have made notes and outlines and drafted leads and key sections of text, I do not look at them as I begin to write. Each step made the next one possible, each expedition into the unknown develops its own track.

Of course I repeat myself, but, I hope, in a different way. I approach the subject from a new direction, define the problem in new terms, develop it with the tool of a new metaphor. I write fast, hoping for connections that would never logically concern me.

The reason I write is simple: to surprise myself.

I want to discover what I know that I didn't know I knew, to see a familiar subject in an unfamiliar way, to contradict my most certain beliefs, to burst through expectation and intent to insight and clarity, to hurt and laugh and understand and be confused in a way that I have not experienced before. Bobbie Ann Mason talks of "the not knowing that leads you to the knowing," and the composer Lukas Foss says, "Creation is the surprise that in retrospect makes sense."

My writing may reach others, and I hope it does. I want to inform, persuade, entertain, celebrate. But my first audience is myself. Many other writers have testified to this. Toni Cade Bambara says, "First and foremost I write for myself. Writing has been for a long time my major tool for self-instruction and self-development." Edward Albee says, "I write for me. For the audience of me." Mekeel McBride states, "In early drafts, a poem is for me. After that, it's for anyone, everyone."

Surprise is the product of awareness. Elizabeth Bowen explains, "The writer . . . sees what he did not expect to see . . . Inattentive learner in the schoolroom of life, he keeps some faculty free to hear and wonder. His is the roving eye. By that roving eye is his subject found. The glance, at first only vaguely caught, goes on to concentrate, deepen; becomes the vision."

The writer's eye captures the extraordinary in the ordinary. I am never bored. Waiting for my wife in the supermarket, waiting for a meeting to begin, standing in line at the post office, sitting off to the edge of a cocktail party, sitting in my car waiting for the drawbridge to lower, I observe the world.

What are people doing? Why? What are they not doing? Why? What was this like a hundred years ago? What will it be like a hundred years from now? What are the most specific details I can spot? What do they reveal? Which specifics connect? What does their pattern reveal? What specifics repel others? What does that lack of pattern reveal? What is different from the last time? What is different from expectation? What do I see differently if I move a few inches left or right, farther away or closer in? What would I focus on if this were a movie scene? What would I emphasize in a sketch? What am I learning? What would somebody else need to learn? The questions reel on as I store away information that may, days later, years later, connect in a way that surprises.

I encourage surprise while writing a draft by writing so that I run ahead of my self-censor and so that my speed causes the informative accidents of insight and language that teach me what the evolving pages know. "How do I know what I think until I see what I say?" asks E. M. Forster; "We write about what we don't know about what we know," states Grace Paley.

The process of reading surprise continues when I revise and edit. During revision, I re-see the subject, developing clues into understandings, hints into insights, reordering to produce clearer patterns, each draft an adventure into meaning.

That process narrows but continues during editing; a cut clarifies, a phrase moved changes emphasis, sentences or paragraphs connected or broken apart make me see and hear what I have to say. Even a change from a comma to a dash can increase my understanding of my subject.

I read not what I *expect* to appear on the page but what *is* on the page. This failure of intent opens a moment of possibility and I plunge through, discovering what I have said and what I need to say.

How to Recognize Surprise

All of us experience surprise: a familiar landmark disappears, a friend reveals an attitude that shocks us, a family member behaves in an unexpected way, a medical news story contradicts a therapy we counted on, we have a discomforting or traitorous thought, or we experience a strange emotional reaction to a normal situation.

The line. I usually experience surprise in a line, a fragment of language that contains a tension I explore or release by writing. These lines are often in a private language that would not mean anything to someone else: "can listen to oboe" after hearing an Albinoni piece our daughter Lee played. Lee died eighteen years ago. If I wrote about this I might discover that I have experienced a healing that would please Lee. Few people who encounter that line in my daybook would have any idea what it is about. But if I am to recognize surprise, I need to be tuned to my own thoughts and feelings.

The external line. Most of my writing begins with an external line. These come unbidden while I am living my life. Some of my recent columns come from such lines: "stress comes before test," "historians' war not mine,"

"In August, Floridians fear hurricanes, New Englanders fear house guests," "the grandchildren are coming, the grandchildren are coming."

Usually I write these lines down in my daybook, on one of the 3" x 5" cards, or on the pad on my car dashboard; sometimes they just stick in my mind. Occasionally I will go to a computer file and write the line out as a lead, perhaps even follow it for a few more lines. The house guest line became such a lead, but when I pursued it the column became a tribute to good house guests and why they were good.

The line is so important to me that I will not begin a piece of writing without one that contains a tension that will drive the piece forward. I may brainstorm specifics about a subject I have been assigned by an editor or by myself, listing what comes into my head, noticing what is unexpected, what specifics connect or relate to each other, especially when there is tension in that relationship.

If I were to be assigned to write a Christmas piece, I would start brainstorming:

No pillow or white beard needed, now I look like Santa
Reindeer we saw in Lapland
Ate Donner and Blitzen
Tree we picked out after Lee died
Why gave home to ugliest tree no one else would buy
Christmas dinner in combat
We were turkeys being fattened for the kill
Goose or turkey
Roast beef
Sauerkraut? At Christmas dinner
Dog who opened family's presents
Carols
Getting not giving is Christmas game
Deacon father in retail business
Profits not prophets
Bad boy lump of coal in Christmas
Mother's fear—anxiety?—about Christmas

My ideas are usually rooted in the specific and grow from a close examination of a specific or two caught in a line.

The internal line. What I didn't understand until recently was the crucial role the line plays in the writing of the piece. I found that I progress through a draft, working from surprise to surprise the way a rock climber moves from handhold to toehold to handhold. The internal lines tell me what the draft has to say, where it develops additional and unexpected meanings that expand and support the potential meaning of the original line.

We should remember how ordinary the line is and not look for a grand theory or spectacular idea. The commonplace—or two commonplaces rubbing together—reveals what we should explore next in writing. During the drafting, the writer might not be consciously aware of what is happening. I choose to explore the process of writing and so make myself aware of what is going on, but other writers do not need this technical awareness if the writing is going well. If it is not going well they may need to look at their own writing practice or the practices of others. The writer normally should be lost in the act of writing; the writer's attention should be totally engaged with seeing, experiencing the subject.

Writing fast encourages surprise; velocity produces the lines that stimulate the next chunk of writing. (The lines that surprise the writer and keep him or her writing are not necessarily the lines that will surprise an individual reader and keep him or her reading.) Here is the case history of the column that came from the line, "stress comes before the test."

> The doctor has ordered a stress test, but it should be called a post-stress test.
>
> This is routine. No new symptoms (that I know of) just a chronological test based on the number of years since the by-pass. He explains all that and I nod.
>
> Then I catch him in the corridor, tell him I'm not worried if I have to have another by-pass operation [not much!], wonder if he will do something with a laser instead of cutting, use that chemical blasting technique I've read about—perhaps a rotorooter . . .
>
> "Let's wait until we see the results of the test," he says, clutching my medical file to his breast and back pedaling.
>
> "I'm not worried," I reassure him, "*just intellectually curious.*"

The line in italics suprised me because it was so obviously dishonest, yet true. That line indicated that the "serious" column I was writing out of terror was going to have a somewhat humorous tone.

> He smiles that doctor's smile and looks pleadingly over my shoulder to the nurse who leads me away to make the appointment for the test.
>
> As if they had to set up an appointment to induce stress. Long before I get to the hospital I will have survived pre-test stress. I will have dreamt, fantasized, imagined everything that could happen, that could be discovered—and more.

The treadmill will run backwards and my *hips will be rotated*

With this line I have almost passed into a surreal world—and, of course, such medical adventures are, in part, surreal. I carry my anxieties to the limit and in that way both explore and defuse my terror—and, I hope, the reader's. I have to keep writing to see where the draft will take me.

so that for the rest of my life my feet will point behind me and I'll have to walk using those little mirrors bike riders use on their spectacles.

The thallium will make my beard polka dot.

I'll go so fast that the bottom of my running shoes will catch on fire and my feet will be welded to the treadmill.

They will find that all my arteries are blocked but the blood is flowing just fine through my bones and I'll be written up in the medical journals and be interviewed on television by Dr. Timothy Johnson.

The x-rays of my heart will reveal all my *sins of omission*,

This line takes me beyond the physical.

organized in alphabetical order.

- Letitia, aunt, letter thanking for birthday Indian head dress in 1932 when I was eight years old not written.
- Wordsworth, british poet, footnote references to critical articles on college paper on which I received "a" exposed as made up at 2:11 am, may 12, 1947.

Of course the idea that stress has to be induced by a contraption in a hospital laboratory is ridiculous. Life produces stress the doctor could test if he would give up the golf course and follow me around for an hour or two.

There is the stress when I order my bagel "not toasted, please" and watch it flipped into the toaster. There is the stress of eating a toasted bagel when you ordered a non-toasted one. There is the stress of wondering why you did not leap up on the counter and demand a non-toasted bagel.

And the stress of restraining your natural response when you ask for "black coffee, please" and the person at the counter asks, "yuh want cream in it?"

And the stress of the car that passes on the right signaling an intimate salute because of my "over 60" vanity plates and the dignity of my driving style.

The stress when Minnie Mae says, "where do you want to eat?" then makes gagging noises when I suggest my favorite restaurant.

What the stress test will show is that I'm a master of stress. If there is no stress in my life, I go out and create some.

I arrive early at lunch and feel stress because my companion is 37 seconds late; I suffer stress because I can't find a parking place and I'm only two minutes early for lunch.

I feel the stress of rejection when I don't get any mail; the stress of having to answer letters when I do.

Stress boils up my esophagus when I am not invited to a dinner party—or when I am invited and have to accept.

The other day, sitting in my favorite chair, listening to the Mozart clarinet quintet, I realized I felt funny. Ever the alert cardiac patient, I took account of my condition.

My heart beat was regular. I had no chest pains. My head did not hurt. My stomach did not burn. My hand did not tremble. I felt no righteous anger. I had no complaint. No worry. No fears. No anxiety. No stress.

That strange, funny feeling was content.

I fell asleep.

I dreamt I was taking my stress test. I felt no stress. They cranked up the treadmill until the motor smoked. My feet danced along. My heart rate stayed normal, my breathing was even, I wore the smile of zen upon my face.

The doctor

I don't know where the piece is taking me. It is an amusing and varied listing but it must arrive at a destination. Then I write the line "the doctor" and I have a place to go. I can express what the parient feels toward the people ordering and running the test.

started breathing deeply, his face got red, his legs became rubbery, he clutched his chest.

I smiled, running on and on.

Image. The other principal way surprise comes to me is through the image. When you ask young children to show you their writing, they are as likely to show you a drawing as they are to show you words on paper. Most writers stay in that state although they keep the pictures a secret. Surprise comes to me visually. Columns have come to me when I have seen in the world, in memory, on the screen or museum wall, with my mind's eye, an image that serves me as well as a line does. Recently I

watched our house rotate on a turntable so it faced the woods instead of the road, and that image led to a column about winterizing our back porch. I saw myself dancing my last high-school dance in my overcoat in 1942 and found a column about the mysteries of sex long before the sexual revolution.

Many writers I know might have been artists if they had had a different art teacher. That was certainly true for me. I think it is important to return to the important works of art that govern how we see, and to keep looking at the world in a way that evokes surprise.

The Common Forms of Surprise

The poet A. E. Housman said, "...I could no more define poetry than a terrier can define a rat but that I thought we both recognized the object by the symptoms which it provokes in us... Experience has taught me, when I am shaving of a morning, to keep watch over my thoughts, because, if a line of poetry strays into my memory, my skin bristles so that the razor ceases to act."

Perhaps because I have a beard, my surprise is not so dramatic—but it is instinctive. Looking back, however, I think my instincts are sparked by seven forms of surprise.

A connection. I am writing and I remember my three-year-old grandson's description of himself—"I hero"—and that connects so quickly with a foolish "hero" who died close to me in combat where we used the term sarcastically. This connection must be explored by writing.

A tension. There are many forms of tension—what is and what should be, what is and what will be, what is in conflict with something else. Every time I sense a tension, I examine it carefully. Look at the tension between the two concepts of hero: one by a three-year-old grandson fascinated by Batman and one held by his grandfather who survived "heroic" combat. Another tension I had to deal with in my childhood was between my parents' warnings against the "heathen" Irish Catholics and the Irish Catholic mothers in my neighborhood who were able to give me the affection my own mother could not. That tension of childhood that still produces writing at age seventy.

Contradiction. I often joke that I didn't know the difference between prophets and profits as a child, but there was significant contradiction between the religious celebration of Christmas and Easter in an evangelical family and the fact that my father's success in the store was based on Christmas and Easter sales.

An unexpected word, line, or image. I describe a person I know and respect when I find myself writing the word *nice* instead of *good* and realize the unexpected difference that is true to my subject, or write that she faced life with an aggressive goodness and begin to understand why people reacted to her as they did, or I see a mental picture of her face looking self-satisfied—almost smug—as she does good and realize there is a complex person behind the mask of goodness taught in her family.

A problem. I listen to a friend talk and realize that the problem is not so much how badly he's treated by his boss as that he allows his boss to know he fears him. I begin to wonder if fear among men invites bad treatment, and realize I have a piece about corporate life I might explore.

A question. Robert Cormier explains, "What if? What if? My mind raced, and my emotions kept pace at the sidelines, the way it always happens when a story idea arrives, like a small explosion of thought and feeling. What if? What if an incident like that in the park had been crucial to a relationship between father and daughter? What would make it crucial? Well, what if the father, say, was divorced from the child's mother and the incident happened during one of his visiting days? And what if . . . "

Increased honesty. Most of all, effective writing comes when we confront our subject with honesty, finding true—and unexpected—moments of honesty: the joy I felt in combat, the anger at my daughter for her dying.

Each of us has had a boss who says, "Don't surprise me." That may be legitimate counsel in certain situations, but the writer is the person who seeks surprise even—perhaps especially—when it is uncomfortable. E. L. Doctorow says, "Everytime you compose a book your composition of yourself is at risk. You put yourself further away from whatever is comfortable to you or you feel at home with. Writing is a lifetime act of self-displacement." It is in our discomfort that we find the truths of our subjects and our lives that need exposure and celebration.

And so, in my seventies, I still find myself waking at 5:30 or earlier in the morning so I can get to my desk and write what I do not expect. I invite, encourage, cultivate, welcome and follow surprise.

3

Trying on the Essay

Exploring Personal Experience

When I was in college my professors preached an aesthetic pyramid of literature: poetry at the peak, fiction and drama below, nonfiction at the bottom. I bought it. I wrote nonfiction, essays and articles, and aspired to write poetry and fiction. I undervalued the essays I wrote, thinking they were not literature. But fashions change and today the genres seem more equal; in fact, the personal essay seems to be achieving artistic equality. This change is due largely to the political climate in which literature is published and taught. The women's movement and the encouragement of diversity invited personal experience, personal opinion, and personal voices. Those voices often speak in essays that explore what had been secret, unspoken emotional and intellectual responses to life. I have many reasons to write the personal essay.

- The artist's answer, nothing less: to give voice to those without a voice, to articulate the unspoken feelings and thoughts of the reader.
- To give myself voice. I am heard when I write; I vote in the human community, registering my opinions, what I stand for, what I fear, what I stand against, what I celebrate.
- To discover who I am. Writing the personal essay celebrates my difference, authenticates who I am, justifies my existence.
- Hearing myself allows me to hear others. The farther I go into myself, the more I can enter into the lives of others; the more I

enter the lives of those different from me, the more I understand myself.

- The personal essay allows me to report the important news of the human condition, the stories rarely covered on page one, on radio news, on television.
- I discover how much I know that I didn't know I knew. Writing educates me.
- Writing the personal essay allows me to make use of my experience. I explore the lives I have lived and am living, even those I may live in the future.
- Donald Barthelme told us to "write about what you're most afraid of." When I do, I survive the terrors that silence me. While writing, the dark clouds rise, the monster shadows retreat. Graham Greene explains, "Writing is a form of therapy; sometimes I wonder how all those who do not write, compose or paint can manage to escape the madness, the melancholia, the panic fear which is inherent in the human situation." Writing is my therapy.
- Writing the personal essay is a favorite form of play. I laugh as a sentence turns toward an unexpected meaning, chuckle as the wrong word becomes the right word, grin as the lie becomes the truth.
- I write the personal essay because I will never learn how to write the personal essay, an art that—blessedly—can never be learned. As I grow old, I am forever a young apprentice to my craft.

These are reasons to write in any genre but I think it is important to recognize how the writer's—and the reader's—needs are satisfied by the essay. I think of my columns as essays, a private conversation with each reader. It is a form I love to write, and after publishing nearly four hundred of these conversations I still find the essay provides me with a great variety of forms and voices. In the essay of personal experience, an individual writer speaks to an individual reader, imagines a reader's response and responds to it. Writer and reader explore the topic together. Writing the essay is an intimate art that can include the entire range of human conversation.

Essays can argue, mourn, describe, analyze, make fun, propose, persuade, record, entertain, irritate, inspire, discourage, confide, share, explain, document, criticize, celebrate. In the essay, the writer sits on a bench beside the reader and comments on the life they share.

I was taught a distinction between the formal and the informal essay, but today almost all essays are written in an informal voice. Many of the essays I studied in school—especially those by Emerson and Stevenson—discussed intellectual or moral issues from a distance. I was far more serious, and far more interested in imposing my morality on others, when I was young; and I liked these essays then. I still respect them but I grew to love the essays of Montaigne, Orwell, E. B. White and Didion because they were personal. They made themselves their own subject, placing personal experience in a wider context. These essays seemed written for themselves, then shared with others; they seemed written not to argue some position that had already been taken but were written to explore experience and discover a potential meaning.

At first, most writers just write personal narratives—the fishing trip with father, the birth of a child, the divorce, the death of a grandparent. These are not essays; they are simple, chronological accounts. The material can make these narratives moving, especially to the teacher or friend with whom they are shared, but the writer needs to make the next step, turning this narrative into a personal essay. The essay looks at narrative experience critically—empathetically but evaluative—putting experience in a larger context, trying on the patterns of meaning hidden within the experience. This is critical thinking; the essay takes a broad experience and narrows it down so that it can be examined, or takes a narrow experience and discovers the broader issues that lie within it. These explorations are good therapy for the writer and, if shared or published, for the reader.

The essay is usually the best way for a beginner to enter the writer's world, for it allows the writer to relive a personal experience of importance to the writer and discover a context and pattern of meaning that will make it significant to a reader.

The Hint of a Topic

The essayist is constantly alert to the world and to the writer's personal reaction to that world. As one who publishes a weekly essay, I am never bored. I remember Henry James' counsel: "Try to be one of those people on whom nothing is lost." I observe, overhear, remember, imagine, but equally important, I am alert to my own reaction and respect it even if it makes me uncomfortable. Most people seem to suspect their individual reactions, particularly if they seem to disagree with those around them, but writers know their difference is their strength.

That difference is sparked when a clue for an essay comes from an image caught out of the corner of the eye, a fleeting half-thought, an almost feeling that is not yet understood. I catch a glimpse of myself in the reflection of a black, night window and see my mother's aging, heavy step. I feel the killing violence I used in war rise within me when a car cuts me off in traffic. I see a high-school rebel in purple, spiked hair and myself in the zoot suit that so satisfyingly worried my parents. I wonder, during Christmas dinner when everyone appears happy, why I remove myself psychologically and observe the festivities from a great distance.

The Instigating Line

What I see—and what I think and feel about it—often scares, contradicts, amuses, angers, intrigues me so that I write to discover its meaning. This tension between what I expect to think or feel and what I actually think or feel is usually caught in a line, the fragment of language filled with potential that we discussed in the last chapter. The line is so important that it must be emphasized here again. The line may be overlooked by the inexperienced writer because the words seem ordinary.

These lines are hardly topics. They are not as developed as that. The development comes in the writing. The line, "Tell me a story, Daddy" reminds me that my daughters always wanted to hear the old, familiar stories and that sparks a column on how I like to read series of mysteries in which the detectives, their worlds, and the crimes they solve are familiar. The word *consultant* pops into my head as during a Christmas visit by a daughter, her husband and their two boys. I write a column defining the role of grandparent by comparing it to the role of corporate consultant I played in another life. "I was born in the laxative age" gave me a black-humor column on the medical world of the aging.

Sometimes the line is an image. I see myself sledding down Wollaston Hill, a small boy held between an uncle's knees; I see Michelle, the little girl who played with her dolls at my side, during street combat in Belgium fifty years ago; I see the trees bent by the prevailing wind that I remember from my first visit to the island of Nantucket. Each of these images contains the seed of writing.

The Lead

Sometimes the line is the lead or first sentence of the essay, the one that sets the tone for all that follows. The beginning of the essay should contain—or strongly imply—a central tension (contradiction, irony, surprise, or problem) that will be explored in the essay. The lead is a promise to readers that they and the writer will discover something during the reading that will make them view the world differently from the way they have in the past.

George Orwell is the master of the essay I most often turned to for inspiration and instruction when I began to write editorials almost half a century ago. I copied out some of the things he said about essay writing:

> So long as I remain alive and well I shall continue to feel strongly about prose style, to love the surface of the earth, and to take a pleasure in solid objects and scraps of useless information.
>
> * * *
>
> Good writing is like a window pane.
>
> * * *
>
> (i) Never use a metaphor, simile or other figure of speech which you are used to seeing in print.
>
> (ii) Never use a long word where a short one will do.
>
> (iii) If it is possible to cut a word out, always cut it out.
>
> (iv) Never use the passive where you can use the active.
>
> (v) Never use a foreign phrase, a scientific word or jargon word if you can think of an everyday English equivalent.
>
> (vi) Break any of these rules sooner than say anything barbarous.
>
> * * *
>
> A scrupulous writer, in every sentence that he writes, will ask himself at least four questions, thus: What am I trying to say? What words will express it? What image or idiom will make it clearer? Is this image fresh enough to have an effect? And he will probably ask himself two more: Could I put it more shortly? Have I said anything that is avoidably ugly?

In preparing to write this chapter I started searching for Orwell's opening lines which I admired. I remembered them as being unexpected but true to what happens in the essay. They tease—and deliver. I hear Orwell's voice invite the reader to stand beside him and see the world as he sees it—with an uncomfortable honesty, a biting wit, and a skepticism that is balanced by compassion, but when I went through his collected works I was surprised at how the first sentences of hundreds of his essays were quite ordinary. My surprise made me want to explore the subject and the result is the following column that, I believe, offers a special comfort to the beginning writer.

> The other morning, when my words lay sodden on the page, I once more apprenticed myself to George Orwell. I search through the pages of my *Collected Essays, Journalism and Letters of George Orwell* by Sonia Orwell and Ian Angus [Harcourt, Brace & World, 1968] seeking instruction and inspiration from such essays as:
>
> *England Your England*
>
> "As I write, highly civilized human beings are flying overhead, trying to kill me."
>
> *Marrakech*
>
> "As the corpse went past the flies left the restaurant table in a cloud and rushed after it, but they came back a few minutes later."
>
> *Reflections on Ghandi*
>
> "Saints should always be judged guilty until they are proved innocent."
>
> *Shooting an Elephant*
>
> "In Moulmein, in Lower Burma, I was hated by large numbers of people—the only time in my life that I have been important enough for this to happen to me."
>
> I was instructed and inspired, but not in the way I expected. In tracking down the famous openings of these essays in the 2,014 pages of the collection, I read dozens of beginnings that were as limp or clumsy as mine. I'm no George Orwell, but neither was George Orwell most days.
>
> We need to remember that our friend's house, neat for company, was ripe with old newspapers, dog hair and a cardboard pizza coffin the night before. Most of us measure our worst against another's best.
>
> A friend of mine once played golf with Ben Hogan in his prime and was surprised that their score was close. It was after the game that he noticed the difference between them. Hogan took four hundred golf balls and hit a hundred on each of four key shots he had missed.
>
> George Orwell not only wrote great essays because of talent honed by craft, but because he wrote. He filled the page, day after day, year after year, practicing his craft so that he was prepared for inspiration when it dropped by.
>
> He also submitted and published the worst while waiting for the best.

Many of us in retirement have the time to pursue our dreams, but we have to relearn the lessons of the crafts that are paying for our retirement.

We have to remember the miles of visits that produced no sales as well as the few visits that paid off; we have to remember the loaves of bread that did not rise before the one that did.

These days I am the poet I wanted to be at eighteen. Now I write the poems I imagined for most of the decades between college and retirement, but not many get in the mail. And if they are not in the mail, they are not rejected—or published.

In retirement I wanted to become the artist I never was. I have shelf after shelf of books on art; drawers filled with pens, pencils, brushes, paints, crayons, charcoal, watercolors, oils; stacks of sketchbooks, paper, canvas.

What I do not have is stacks of drawings and paintings. I haven't found—made—the time.

And as writer I know that talent depends on abundance, the accumulation of work that is good and bad.

In fact, Orwell may not have liked the essays I most admire and been most proud of some of those I pass as ordinary.

The artist often does not know what the world will like. The symphony the composer sees as a failure because it did not achieve his ambition for it, may be the one that is played long after he is gone.

The painting, the play, the book, the newspaper column the maker likes the best may be ignored while the work that is struck off in haste—after a lifetime of apprenticeship to the maker's craft—may be the one that is remembered.

That used to disturb me, but now it offers comfort. The true satisfaction is in the making of the work.

At the moment of making, the writer, painter, composer, golfer, fisherman, baker, quiltmaker enjoy the gift of concentration. And as we age, that gift increases in importance.

We are fortunate when we are lost to the world and too old to suffer the ambition of fame. We are blessed, as Orwell was, when we focus on the small, immediate demands of the work at hand.

This stitch, this dough, this cast, this drive, this melody, this line, this word becomes our momentary universe.

Orwell wasn't, with such a moment, the famous writer, but simply a writer trying to find the right word and fit it into a line that made meaning clear.

And I do not have to be George Orwell any more than he had to be George Orwell. All I have to do is to concentrate on this line, then the next.

Length

That column was 793 words long, just under the ideal length for a newspaper essay that might be published on the op ed page (eight-hundred words), the page that is opposite the editorials in most newspapers. The op ed page editor often buys freelance articles, and it is an ideal place for writers to have their voices heard. Essays in magazines can run two or three times as long, but brevity is an advantage in getting an essay published.

The writer must make sure every word, and every pause between words, contributes to the essay. For years I had the following quotation from William Strunk as reported by E. B. White above my desk until it was tattooed inside my forehead:

> Vigorous writing is concise. A sentence should contain no unnecessary words, a paragraph no unnecessary sentences, for the same reason that a drawing should have no unnecessary lines and a machine no unnecessary parts. This requires not that the writer make all his sentences short, or that he avoid all detail and treat his subjects only in outline, but that every word tell.

Selection

Brevity is achieved by selection. In an essay, the writer focuses on one dominant issue, and everything—each statistic, quotation, fact, anecdote, reference, idea, paragraph, sentence, clause, word—must move the essay forward, contributing to its meaning.

The professional limits the subject far more radically than the amateur: not "*education*," not "*education in the United States*," not "*English education in New Hampshire*," not "*writing in Dick Tappen's classroom*," but "*why Dick Tappen's students write what they fear*." The essay's limited focus allows the writer to explore one topic in depth and give the reader a full and satisfying development of the essay's meaning.

Specific Information

The essay is written like poetry, technical writing, fiction, science writing—with specific information. The tone may be conversational but the reader will not read it unless there is an adequate delivery of information to satisfy the reader's hunger for specifics.

The Common World

In an essay, writer and reader meet in a common world, a familiar country of experience or ideas that they already share but becomes new during the essay. The writer creates this common world with specific details they share, what they do when they are talking on the telephone that the other person cannot see, how they behave in the false privacy of their car in a traffic jam, what they eat in their laps while watching television. The essay writer deals in the commonplace but, then, because of the writer's point of view, the reader sees it anew.

The writer observes and responds to the shared world—what you really think at the funeral, what you think of people who look like their pets, how you can tell when a marriage won't last. The writer weaves a new vision of this shared world by seeing, as if for the first time, what has become ordinary. The essay articulates thoughts and reactions the reader was not previously conscious of; but when read, strike the reader as true.

Trust

The writer's authority is established by the accuracy of the revealing details and the insight and perception of the writer's vision. The reader believes this person sees their common world in such a way that the reader had better pay attention.

In all writing, even technical or scholarly writing, authority may be supported by citations from external sources, but the reader trusts the authority that comes internally from the writer who delivers information or commentary that sparks the shock of recognition within the reader who says, "Yes. That's the way it is. The writer knows what I have been through, how and what I think and feel about it. I'll read more."

Voice

An essay is a conversation, so the reader should hear the individual voice of the writer. The writer should put this heard quality in the writing by writing out loud, tuning the draft by ear to the purpose and meaning of the text. This doesn't mean that all essay writing should be informal or colloquial; it does mean that the music of the text should support the meaning of the draft.

Self-Exposure

In effective writing and, especially in personal-essay writing, the author exposes himself or herself, revealing thoughts and feelings that the reader has also experienced but may have denied. The writer articulates these hidden or suppressed thoughts and feelings, and that is the strength of many essays. It is, however, a problem for the writer who is usually uncomfortable about this self-exposure.

After the death of my daughter, the doctor who had treated her urged me to write about this experience, and my family agreed. I didn't think I would. It was too private, but with their support I have written about it when it seemed necessary or appropriate. Early on, when writing in public during a teacher workshop, a professor accused me of exploiting my daughter's death. This was both a horrible and liberating experience. His charges somehow freed me of the suspicion that I was doing just that. When I have written an essay about my daughter, the response of readers tells me that I am helping them by articulating what they have not been able to say about their own losses.

Editing

Economist John Kenneth Galbraith once said, "... when I'm greatly inspired, only four revisions are needed before, as I've often said, I put in that note of spontaneity which even my meanest critics concede." The essay should be edited out loud, with the writer pacing the writing so the essay builds to points of emphasis and then slows down so the reader can absorb what has been said and be prepared for what will be said.

The final editing should make the draft spontaneous: the murderer carefully raking the ground where the body is buried to hide any sign of struggle. The writing should be deceptively easy to read.

Closing

The ending of an essay should not preach, telling readers what to think—or summarize what the writer thought or discovered—but invite readers to do their own thinking, inspired by the voyage of meaning writer and reader have just shared.

Finding a Context

The primary reason we write—and read—is to find what Robert Frost described as "a momentary stay against confusion." We tolerate a great deal of conflict, disorder and contradiction in our lives, but we turn to art to discover meaning (maybe not *the* meaning, but at least a meaning). It is the primary task of the writer to find a significant meaning or pattern that neither oversimplifies nor confuses.

The search for meaning in experience through writing is essential for all forms of writing, but it is especially appropriate for the personal experience essay. Let me take a snapshot from the memory of my childhood that has produced published writing and see how meaning can grow from experience.

This is what passed through my head and might have been written in my daybook:

> When I was a kid, we once lived in a neighborhood where the guy next door, he was a butcher I think, used to chase his wife around the block waving a cleaver.

If I stop there, you will ask, "So what?" My story isn't a story—yet. It's not an anecdote, not a parable, not a narrative, not an essay, not a poem, not a news story. It is a fragment from a writer's experience inventory, just a note that has action and the potential for drama, even for many meanings. It is a serving of prose without a context. It has no history, no future, no meaningful connection to the writer—or a reader, yet.

Readers often think material comes to the writer pure and complete. They imagine that my memory of the butcher next door instantly becomes a novel that could be described in a listing similar to one in the *TV Guide*: "The Butcher's Wife," the story of a woman who butchered her husband and found God.

The process of making meaning from memory is complex and mysterious. We sit down to write, and instead of what we planned, an image—the light glinting off the cleaver—passes in front of our eyes sixty years after it happened. Graham Greene said, "When I construct a scene, I don't describe the hundredth part of what I see; I see the characters scratching their noses, walking about, tilting back in their chairs—even after I've finished writing—so much so that after a while I feel a weariness that does not derive all that much from my effort of imagination but is more like a visual fatigue: My eyes are tired from watching my characters."

Before writing and during writing I see far more than I can record. And the more I see, the more there is to see as I pass from this world to the remembered or imagined world. We may have forgotten that place, that time, that event, those people, but during writing it is all recreated in enormous detail. Here is something of what appears in my mind's eye when the light glints off that butcher cleaver. These are not clarified thoughts, just fragments in which meaning may be found.

The fragments need a context that surrounds a fragment of writing and gives it meaning. The writer most often begins with the specific rather than the general. The meaning is organic, it grows from the seed of memory.

When the O. J. Simpson story broke and we heard the police tapes of his wife's cries for help, I found myself thinking back on that scene on Vassell Street so many years before. I wrote a simple description of that memory that now had a context and the description grew into a column that was published in the *Boston Globe.*

> When I was a child families sat on the front porch of a Saturday evening and watched neighbors stroll past.
>
> But I remember the time the strolling became a race. The woman next door ran out of the house screaming, followed by her husband, a butcher, waving his cleaver. They circled the block, then went back into the home.
>
> I don't remember police cars. I don't remember any of the men attempting to stop him. I do remember laughter, jokes, explanations: That was the way of "those" people who were not Scotch or Irish, that was typical of "their" religion.
>
> I remembered those races around the block as people cheered O. J. Simpson on during his run from reality along the Freeway.
>
> And then, of course, I heard people say that this was more evidence times have changed for the worse.
>
> They haven't.
>
> Wife beating wasn't approved of in my family, but it existed. And nothing was done about it. It wasn't nice, but no one called the police when, at the Sunday dinner table after church, a husband ordered his wife upstairs, when he removed his belt as he followed her, while everyone at the dinner table heard the belt strike again, again, again.
>
> We were a good Christian family. We kept our shades properly drawn, we went to church, we kept our family secrets secret.

> I feel a sense of betrayal as I write this, but it is time to stop the secrecy. The reason we kept this secret is because, at some level, we believed the husband had a right—more than that, a duty—to maintain order in his house.
>
> My family and others like us kept the secret of wife beating. In our day, women had nowhere to go. Leaving your husband proved you were not a good wife. Churches and temples and even colleagues did not approve of divorce.
>
> And where could a wife who married soon after high school, and had only a limited education and no job skills, go? There were few jobs for women. Women were married for life, were economically dependent, and were duty bound. If they were beaten, they must not have served well.
>
> How many times did police need to be called to Nicole Simpson's house before something was done? O. J. Simpson didn't have special treatment because he was a celebrity; he was treated well because he was a man and an ex-husband who said he wanted reconciliation.
>
> The morning after his arrest I heard some men, men considered good and kind, actually speculating on what O. J.'s wife had done to cause the battering.
>
> But in a strange way I am heartened by the Simpson case. In the global village, the Juice was a member of our family. And now the family secret is out.
>
> Three in every ten women murdered in this country are killed by their husbands or boyfriends. Wife battering is the leading cause of injury among women. And the men who commit these crimes are often men of status, who appear respectable, cool, successful, in control of their lives. They are even members of our family.
>
> Perhaps the Simpson case will make us call the police, perhaps the police will act sooner, perhaps the courts will sentence to the full extent of the law, perhaps we will honestly examine our families and ourselves.
>
> Perhaps we will get help before the police need to be called.

In that case the context stimulated the memory and caused me to make use of it. Years earlier I was writing a poem about the dreadful family dinners of my childhood and the context evolved from the draft that gathered the scene with the butcher from my memory. The title came after a number of drafts, after I had found a meaning in the experience I certainly did not expect.

I ENVY THE BUTCHER'S DAUGHTER

I slide under the table at Sunday dinner,
seeking exile. I have just learned to read
the unsaid, slow turning away, the hesitant
reaching out, quick withdrawal, grown content

with loneliness but fear the roar of uncles,
wived or alone, stranger cousins, jolly voices
unnatural in deacons. Father tells his stories
and they bellow at the familiar pause, nudging

each other as the women gasp. The men compete
for a turkey leg, women for a wing while I hide
cross legged under the table, study the kingdom
of knees, inhale the mystery of women. Even here

I know when the dribble glass leaks, the hinged
spoon spills sugar, watch Uncle Morison sneak
the whoopee cushion onto mother's chair, watch
his knees squeeze the bladder that makes

his new wife's plate rise and fall, hear them wait
for her discomfort, hear their laughter explode.
I hide until family leaves, separateness returns.
Mother leaves the room when Dad comes in, father

flees to the phone. In their wars of silence,
I go to ground. Delivering the evening paper,
I become scholar of lighted windows, collector
of families that remain in the same room.

In summer I pause by open windows, hear cries
of hate, of fear. I envy the butcher's daughter.
Her father, Emil, runs her mother down the block,
light glinting from his shining blade.

In the column I am an adult in a post-feminist era, horrified by domestic violence documented by the tapes on which O. J. Simpson's wife pleads for help. The anecdote from my childhood has a context. In the poem, however, I am concerned with the silent domestic violence within my WASP family and I actually envy the honest emotions I saw as a child in the scene of the butcher chasing his wife around the block. It is the same material set in a very different context.

All writing is autobiographical but it is autobiography placed in context, fragments of experience woven into the ever changing lives we create to understand our lives. As we place our life in significant contexts, as we create the legend or myth of our childhood, our schooling, our war, our profession, our marriage, we are changed. We become the product of our writing.

Don DeLillo says:

> Working at sentences and rhythms is probably the most satisfying thing I do as a writer. I think after a while a writer can begin to know himself through his language. He sees someone or something reflected back at him from these constructions. Over the years it's possible for a writer to shape himself as a human being through the language he uses. I think written language, fiction, goes that deep. He not only sees himself but begins to make himself or remake himself.

As we find meaning in experience, we find ourselves.

Think with a Reader

While I am writing my weekly newspaper column, I often visualize myself sitting beside a friend on a porch or across a table at the Bagelry, drinking coffee, leisurely exploring an idea, a memory, an experience. We speculate, recall, explore, weaving our thoughts and feelings into a conversational tapestry. We do not talk at each other but *with* each other. The personal essay allows us to think with the reader, allowing our ideas to unfold.

My eight hundred words must have more discipline than a rambling conversation, yet I try to achieve the tone of such a conversation, inviting the reader to engage in a dialogue, to think with me. I listen to the reader within me as well as to what I find myself saying. I engage myself in dialogue. I do not know what I will say before I write a column any more than I know what I will say to my breakfast cronies before the conversation stimulates ideas.

I'd like to invite you backstage to observe one of my newspaper columns in the making, listening to the dialogue that took place between myself and my imagined reader.

The column arose because I found myself responding to life in terms of unhappiness I experienced in my childhood. I would bark a response to Minnie Mae that was clearly much stronger than her comment warranted, at a moment of happiness I would feel an inappropriate despair, after a publication I would feel an irrational need for further approval, and in such moments, I have taken to turning inward to examine and understand my behavior. I decided to write my way through this to try to understand my own feelings, and I suspected that if I published this exploration, others of my generation—and some much younger—might find it helpful. The response of readers to this column proved this to be true. I began writing about this, not knowing what I would find myself saying but listening to my reader and exploring the subject *with* my reader.

When my mother-in-law was eight years old her mother sent her to live with an aunt who had a leg amputated. All her long life Katie lorded her rise in social status over her sisters, because she had been brought up in her aunt's large home.

I give the reader information that will touch the reader as it moved me when I first heard it but I hear the reader give a silent, embarrassed "So what?" The reader wonders what this family story has to do with him or her.

But a year before she died at 96 in a nursing home, Katie told a relative that her mother didn't love her, that her mother had given her away.

Now I reveal how my mother-in-law really felt, and again the reader is moved, but also wonders what all this means.

At an age when most of us hoped for serenity, understanding and compassion, I find many over-60s suffering from wounds that have festered for decades.

I put the anecdote, the little story about Katie, in context. The young reader may be surprised, the older reader will recognize the situation. Both, I hope, will nod to encourage me to go on to explain why this is.

Many times we have thought the old hurts and angers had been locked away in the closets of memory, but age brings reflection. Unable or unwilling to look ahead, attempting to live in the moment and failing, we look back.

The reader nods but says, "I thought the old days were better than the present: intact families that stayed together, no violence, no crime."

The young think we yearn for the good old days, but for many of us those days were not so good and, in fact, may have been terrible. As we reflect, the closet door opens and ghosts gallop out. One reason, I suspect, is the new openness about matters that were not spoken of when we were young.

The reader says, "I have two questions: How were the good old days not so good and why are you remembering things you have tried to forget all these years?"

I answer the second question first, saying to the reader, "I'll tell you about the good old days but first let me figure out why we think about them."

Now the unspoken is in the morning newspaper, the weekly magazine, played out in TV series and movies, in obsessive detail on talk shows, brought up in morning coffee or dinner party discussions.

I remind readers of all the talk shows they have seen and point out that this new—and sometimes disgusting openness—allows oldsters to think about what we have been avoiding in our pasts.

Although I am appalled by the public revelations of some matters that I think should remain private, I am in favor of the new openness.

The reader asks, "What do I think of this new openness?" and I say "I am in favor of it," surprising the reader by my answer and making the reader ask a new question: "Why are you in favor of it?"

Far too often sexual abuse—including marital rape, child and wife beatings, and other family crimes—were kept hidden at an awful price. The victim was made to suffer an undeserved guilt, and a situation that should have been stopped continued.

The reader nods in agreement but then asks, hesitantly, "I don't want to invade your privacy, but can you be more specific?"

The situation became dramatic for me one day when I was conferring with a young woman who was trying to write of sexual

I set up the issue of sexual abuse and then the reader asks, "Well, what happened?"

abuse in her childhood. Suddenly I was a child again.

I have often hidden my true feelings with a quip: I was brought up in a dysfunctional family, but it was called a good Christian home in those days.

I avoid the question but set the scene, answering in advance the reader's question, "What kind of a family did you come from?"

I try to bury many painful truths in that line. But they will not stay hidden.

The reader asks, "How won't they stay hidden?"

Minnie Mae does something—or does not do something—and my reaction—hurt, anger, unhappiness—does not come from the present but is in response to my childhood. Someone says something, and I snap back—or retreat into the silence of my childhood. I am not reacting to the now but to the then.

That's how.

"What was then *like?"*

I can remember family incidents from before I was old enough for school that I did not understand, but that I told myself I would understand when I grew up.

I'm not being too specific here but I expect the reader to fill in the blanks with experiences from their own childhood. Then the reader demands, "Be specific."

My grandmother, my mother, my father, my uncles all made this only child their confidant. They talked to me of the most intimate details of marriage and family. I was the listener they needed.

The reader asks, "How did you feel about this?"

I took it all in, enjoying, I expect, the grown-up confidences, the glimpses behind closed doors, the secrets, and the power that such knowledge gave me. My counsel was requested and, I fear, I told each what they wanted to hear, agreeing with what they said because I had nothing else to offer.

A confession that may at first surprise the reader and then the price of this role may dawn on the reader. And the reader asks, "How does that affect you now?"

In my mind I left home years before I escaped to college and military combat, but over sixty I learned that although most of that generation was dead, that childhood was alive within me.

I thought I escaped, but I remind the reader that I said earlier that I return to my childhood. The reader asks, "Did you return with a new, mature understanding?"

And the longer I live my life, pay my bills as they had not, accept people and behaviors they could not, become myself a husband, parent and grandparent, the less, not the more I understand how they lived their lives.

The reader asks, "If not understanding, how about compassion?"

And when I can understand, I often can not achieve the compassion, the forgiveness I hunger for.

"Well, what do you do?"

Recently I have had long talks with grown-ups—some very grown-up—who are still trying to live a life that is not just in response to ambitions and values their parents had for them. Such conversations inspire many an ironic phrase about "family values."

I avoid the reader's question and remind the reader that I am not alone, that may people of my age are in this situation. But the reader asks, "Can't you get help?"

We hope through pastoral counsel, psychological treatment, the understanding of wife or husband, friends and children, to free ourselves of the anger, bitterness, and corrosive guilt that is our inheritance.

I answer by telling the reader where I can turn for help but then the reader says, "But what do you do?"

I try to make peace with the past by reminding myself I live within a life that is so different from my childhood and so much better than I could ever have expected. I confront the ghosts that escape the closet of memory with a fierce honesty and without guilt. I make myself remember the many good values I was given in my childhood.

I tell the reader what I do and the reader presses harder: "Does it help?"

Still I am surprised at the continuing effort it takes to heal the hurts of a childhood lived so very many years ago, a past that is so painfully immediate today.

I answer the reader but echo back to the beginning. Katie tried to escape the painful memories of childhood, could not and neither can we.

This column could have been written from the stance of someone who was cross at people who let childhood events affect their behavior in old age. It could have been a "Buck up and forget it" lecture. This essay depended entirely on personal reflection, but I could also have written a piece based on psychological studies and on the new drugs that help people who suffer paralyzing emotional and mental symptoms. I could have approached the subject in many other ways, but I chose to expose and examine my own behaviors, feelings, thoughts.

I am not always comfortable in doing this, and if the Durham, New Hampshire, police storm into my writing room one morning and charge me with self-exposure, I will not be surprised. But in focusing on myself, I do not threaten my readers; I take my readers along on a journey of self-examination.

I first became fully aware of this stance when I wrote many columns during the Gulf War. I was against the war, but I did not write as a dove attempting to convert hawks, I wrote as a soldier who had been a paratrooper in combat in World War II, and I talked about the experience of combat from the point of view of a veteran, not saying we should or should not be at war in the desert, but pointing out what war was like for me—and, by implication, for others who would be sent to this new war. I did not attack patriotic propaganda, but talked in vivid, first-hand detail of what infantry war is like. The reader response was amazing—and rewarding. Clearly, I reached many who were in favor of the war, opposed to the war, or unclear where they stood on the particular issues in this conflict.

The essay writer invites the reader to stand beside the writer on a promontory and observe the geography of the essay and comment upon it. The writer can be a narrator who objectively reveals a situation, an advocate who is for or against, a historian who puts an immediate concern in perspective, a student of the issue who dissects it, a humorist who points out the ironies or the ridiculousness of the event, a futurist who speculates how the issue will produce change, a pragmatist who reveals what will work and not work, an optimist who celebrates the event or issue. The range of ways the essay writer responds to life is as wonderfully diverse as human response to the individual experience of life.

The most effective essays, I believe, are those that find a way for the writer to reveal a process of thought that invites the reader to think alongside the writer. The writer does not talk down or up to the reader but across to the reader. The master essay writers—Didion, E. B. White, Orwell, Dillard—respect their readers. They do not preach, exhort, attack, but share. Their writing is an invitation to thought.

My first reader, as is the case with most writers, is myself. I must respect myself to write well, accepting my reactions to what I am thinking about in writing without being judgmental, realizing that the most unexpected—even bizarre—reaction to the text may be one worth considering.

When I write I am aware of a community of readers: Minnie Mae who is upstairs, my eldest daughter and her husband in Massachusetts, my youngest daughter and her husband in New York, Chip Scanlan in Florida, Don Graves in the New Hampshire mountains, Elizabeth Cooke in northern Maine, Tom Romano in Ohio, Tom Newkirk across the street, Brock Dethier and Lisa Miller a few miles away, and so many others with whom I share writing. I do not write without feeling their delight when

I turn a clarifying phrase, their laughter at an irony, their nodding approval at a strong reaction to life. This community expands or contracts depending on my subject or my genre. Sometimes I will fax a draft to one of them, or read a few lines out loud over the phone.

It is my audience that helps me decide whether to seek outside documentation, to go to the library and to authorities for instruction and support. I would do this if I felt that my personal experience would not tap into the experience of my readers. If the reader would not grant me authority, then I would seek external authorities to convince the reader.

When I am having difficulty writing an essay, I often imagine a reader outside the invisible writing community that crowds my writing room. I choose an individual I respect but who is not interested in the subject and I talk to that person in my draft.

As we talk in the essay, I adjust my pace to the reader's. If the draft moves too quickly, the reader, walking over the territory of the essay beside the writer, will fall behind; if the writer dawdles, the reader will wander off.

And as we continue our conversation in the essay, I make sure I do not say too much—or too little. How much definition, description, explanation, documentation or evidence does the reader need? Too little and the reader will become uninterested; too much and the reader will be uninterested.

If you write so that the reader thinks with you, readers will take the essay away from you and make it their own. Good. Each of us, writer and reader, come to the essay with all of our individual experience, thoughts, feelings, beliefs. The effective essay causes each reader to create a text that neither belongs to the writer nor the reader, but is created between them. I am often shocked by what my readers have read in my text but I have come to realize that it is not my text but our text. These individual drafts, each one different from the other, are the final evidence that we have thought together.

4

Trying on Fiction

Experiencing Story

Narrative is the mother of all writing. We changed from animal to human beings when we captured, shared, and examined experience in the stories we told and the stories we were told.

Story allows us to bring order to experience, to find pattern in events, to discover meaning in confusion—and story allows us to *share* the order, pattern, meaning. Through story we remember, understand, instruct, entertain, celebrate. The range of all human experience and the intellectual, emotional, and spiritual response to experience is held within story. Stories contain and reveal our beliefs, our fears, our hopes, our knowledge of how the world works.

Narrative underlies our recording of experience. The narrative may be nonfiction, or drama, or poetry. Story is embedded in biography and autobiography, a research paper, a lawyer's brief, an advertisement, a scientific report, a sermon, a love letter. Narrative takes human activity and places it in a meaningful order.

How do we get to know others? By exchanging stories. Courtship does not begin with a kiss but with the sharing of stories; friendship begins when we trust another with our story and we trust that person trusts us enough to offer their story in return. We offer the gift of our own story and accept the gift of the other's story and we may, if the courtship or friendship continues, begin to tell each other all our stories. Corporations and nations negotiate by exchanging stories and making up a new, combined version. Scientists as well as writers create their truths by telling, listening, and creating new stories of how the universe and our physical world within it are changing.

To write stories, we should begin with confidence. We are all familiar with story telling; we heard stories before we could speak and when we had words we started to tell stories. We have read stories and watched stories in life and on stage and screen. Others may be better storytellers in public or have worked at the craft of story telling in coffee shop, class, or at home, but we do not come to the writing of stories innocent of story.

Show, Don't Tell

For all our experience with story, most beginning fiction writers tell *about* the story. The storyteller gets between the reader and the story, telling the reader how to react, how to feel. The craft of fiction allows the writer to reveal the story—to remove the fourth wall of the room—so that the reader enters into the story and experiences it. Writing teachers keep repeating, "Show, don't tell." Mark Twain said, "Don't say the old lady screamed—bring her on and let her scream."

Of course we can all cite short stories and novels in which the author has told rather than shown, but I believe that the beginning writer should build on an understanding of how people and their lives are revealed on the page. In the following scene from *The Man Who Had Everything*, a novel of mine published in 1964, I could have told about the situation. Brad Hastings has suffered an accident and become paralyzed from the neck down. I could have said, "There was a day when his wife had to accept the reality of his condition. Until she and he hit bottom, they could not begin to construct a life of reality. One day she paid a surprise visit to the hospital and could not find him. When she did, she was disheartened to find that he did not even respond to her gift of the jelly doughnuts he had always loved."

Telling the story this way would not affect the reader, who has to become aware of the situation as Bets does. The situation has to be revealed both to the characters and to the reader. It also should be dramatic, with the characters affected and changed by their interaction. The story moves forward on that dramatic energy and it cannot go back. (Bets Hastings is the wife of a newly institutionalized quadriplegic; Brad is the quadriplegic; Carey is a fellow patient.)

> One of those days in the endless chain of days when Bets went shopping as an escape, she realized she couldn't forget Brad and decided to go to

the hospital early. The unexpected impulse reminded her of when they were just married and she would lunch with him in the city. She felt a hint of excitement. She would surprise him—perhaps that would reach him. She would take him some jelly doughnuts—fresh, warm, the way he loved them—and later, carrying the white paper bag, she hurried to his ward and his bed. It was empty.

"Where's Brad?" she asked.

"I don't know," Carey answered. "They took him away."

"For good?" she blurted in panic.

"Oh, no such luck." His voice underlined that what would have been a tragedy for her would have been a comfort to him. "Not for good. He'll be back for supper." Bets wanted to hunt for Brad, but Carey had her trapped. "Isn't that an evil hour for supper four o'clock in the afternoon? Just so they can go home. We don't eat from then until eight the next morning. That's sixteen hours, two-thirds of a day, Mrs. Hastings. No food, not even a snack. They shave us and then, quick as begetting a bastard—beg your pardon—three meals. Breakfast at eight, lunch at eleven, and supper at four—swoosh. Now, you know, I just bet the county commissioners don't realize that."

"I don't suppose they do."

"Would if they visited," he whispered. "Do you know any of their wives socially?"

"I don't believe so."

"Find out," he ordered hoarsely. "Find out. Get 'em to come in and see us."

"I will," Bets promised, seizing the moment of escape, "I will," knowing she wouldn't. The nurse in charge didn't know where Brad was, and Bets was made to realize she didn't care. The nurse's mouth was filled with a cheese Danish and Bets shivered as the creature sloshed in some coffee, tan with cream, and slogged out the words, "Burgie took 'im." But no one knew where Burgie, the half-wit orderly, had gone. Bets hunted through the corridors, ignoring the resentment of patients and staff, looking into wards and offices, examination rooms, day rooms, and down every corridor, realizing that Brad had no control over where he'd been taken—and that she, his wife, had no right to know where he was. She was not wife or nurse, merely a visitor. Running, Bets turned a corner, opened a door, and there he was.

Brad sat in his wheelchair in the center of a vast hall, utterly alone. The room was unlighted, unshadowed, but dark with the gray light of winter, oozing through a few long windows on one side of an unused assembly hall, the windows that were barred and then caged with wire and finally frosted with grime, dark to the sun. Her husband sat unmoving, his body slumped in the canvas wheelchair. His hands lay, palms up, in his lap, useless, the way they had been placed there by some stranger. His face was toward her, but he gave no sign of recognition as she ran, then slowed down and walked across the bare wooden floor, her footsteps the only sound, each step hitting on the echo of her past step. "Jelly doughnuts," she said, her voice too loud in the echoing hall as she lay the white bag on his lap, an offering.

He gave no sign, and she took one out. Obediently her husband opened his mouth, and she broke off a bite and placed it in his mouth and her husband chewed it, slowly, and she broke off another piece and he ate that, dutifully, no pleasure or pain. She was beyond weeping as she bent over, the two of them in the vast hall, and fed her husband a sloppy red jelly doughnut, bite by bite, as she once had fed their children. When she was through, Bets took out a Kleenex and neatly cleaned her husband's chin.

Let's go through it again while I explain what I was doing and why.

One of those days in the endless chain of days when Bets went shopping as an escape, she realized she couldn't forget Brad and decided to go to the hospital early. The unexpected impulse reminded her of when they were just married and she would lunch with him in the city. She felt a hint of excitement. She would surprise him—perhaps that would reach him.

Most beginning writers use the first person: I. *This is natural, but very difficult, for the* I *is not only the narrator but also a character, and it is hard to reveal yourself as a character. The breakthrough to fiction, to showing rather than telling, usually comes when we write in the third person, using* he *or* she. *This gives us distance and helps us to watch the story and report what is happening as it reveals itself. The third person, however, allows the writer to be in a character's mind. In this novel I had chapters in which I was in Bets' mind, experiencing the world with her sensibilities. Other times I was in Brad's mind or the doctor's, Irv Frank, whose surgery caused Brad's paralysis.*

She would take him some jelly doughnuts—fresh, warm, the way he loved them—and later, carrying the white paper bag, she hurried to his ward and his bed. It was empty.

"Where's Brad?" she asked.

We discover the empty bed with Bets and experience her panic.

"I don't know," Carey answered. "They took him away."

We hear what he says and wonder with Bets if he has died or had an accident or been transferred.

"For good?" she blurted in panic.

And now we experience a significant misunderstanding. What is terrible to Bets—and to the reader—would be a blessing to the patient. Remember, I did not plan this reaction. I listened to the character and reported what the character said. I was as surprised as Bets.

"Oh, no such luck." His voice underlined that what would have been a tragedy for her would have been a comfort to him. "Not for good. He'll be back for supper." Bets wanted to hunt for Brad, but Carey had her trapped.

In reading this years after it was written—"what would have been a tragedy for her would have been a comfort to him"—seems heavy handed, an insulting "telling" to the reader as if I didn't have confidence in my writing or the audience's reading.

"Isn't that an evil hour for supper four o'clock in the afternoon? Just so they can go home. We don't eat from then until eight the next morning. That's sixteen hours, two-thirds of a day, Mrs. Hastings. No food, not even a snack. They shave us and then, quick as begetting a bastard—beg your pardon—three meals. Breakfast at eight, lunch at eleven, and supper at four—swoosh. Now, you know, I just bet the county commissioners don't realize that."

"I don't suppose they do."

"Would if they visited," he whispered. "Do you know any of their wives socially?"

"I don't believe so."

"Find out," he ordered hoarsely. "Find out. Get 'em to come in and see us."

"I will," Bets promised, seizing the moment of escape, "I will," knowing she wouldn't. The nurse in charge didn't know where Brad was, and Bets was made to realize she didn't care. The nurse's mouth was filled with a cheese Danish and Bets shivered as the creature sloshed in some coffee, tan with cream, and slogged out the words, "Burgie took 'im." But no one knew where Burgie, the half-wit orderly, had gone. Bets hunted through the corridors, ignoring the resentment of patients and staff, looking into wards and offices, examination rooms, day rooms, and down every corridor, realizing that Brad had no control over where he'd been taken—and that she, his wife, had no right to know where he was. She was not wife or nurse, merely a visitor. Running, Bets turned a corner, opened a door, and there he was.

The dialogue takes us into the county home patient's world.

Brad sat in his wheelchair in the center of a vast hall, utterly alone. The room was unlighted, unshadowed, but dark with the gray light of winter, oozing through a few long windows on one side of an unused assembly hall, the windows that were barred and then caged with wire and finally frosted with grime, dark to the sun. Her husband sat unmoving, his body slumped in the canvas wheelchair. His hands lay, palms up, in his lap, useless, the way they had been placed there by some stranger. His face was toward her, but he gave no sign of recognition as she ran, then slowed down and walked across the bare wooden floor, her footsteps the only sound, each step hitting on the echo of her past step. "Jelly doughnuts," she said, her voice too loud in the echoing hall as she lay the white bag on his lap, an offering.

Brad's institutionalization becomes increasingly clear to Bets. Again, I think I did not need to say, on the previous page, "She didn't care." But I show that Brad has no control over where he is taken. Now I show him. Bets—and the reader—sees him, below, the reader is shown her feeding him and his reaction.

He gave no sign, and she took one out. Obediently her husband opened his mouth, and she broke off a bite and placed it in his mouth and her husband chewed it, slowly, and she broke off another piece and he ate that, dutifully, no pleasure or pain. She was beyond weeping as she bent over, the two of them in the vast hall, and fed her husband a sloppy red jelly doughnut, bite by bite, as she once had fed their children. When she was through, Bets took out a Kleenex and neatly cleaned her husband's chin.

The chapter ends with an action and the reader is not told what it means but is allowed to discover the meaning.

If I have been successful the reader has not been told *about* Brad's stituation, but taken into the county home to observe and experience both Brad and Bets' life in the county home.

Writing the Scene

I think I became capable of writing fiction when I learned how to write a scene. As a former literature major, I was struggling with what seemed destined to be another unfinished novel when someone told me that Joseph Conrad had said, "A novel is written in *scenes of confrontation*." I have hunted for years for the place where Conrad wrote that, but even if he did not, that insight, more than any other, made it possible for me to write and publish fiction.

Most beginning writers, perhaps because we are introverts always imaging what we should have said the night before, start writing with a person alone, reflecting on an event that has taken place off stage. This is a legitimate fictional technique, but most fiction moves forward on the energy that comes from a scene in which one person does something to another person and that person responds. What is done can be a physical action, but the normal action in a scene is dialogue; as Elizabeth Bowen said, "Speech is what the characters *do to each other*." What is said—or not said—cannot be changed, but the person who said it and the one it is said to are changed.

The scene does not tell the reader what happened in the past but allows the event to occur in the presence of the reader. The reader is witness to the action of the story and can decide what is really happening and what its effect will be on the characters.

The scene of confrontation is the basic building block of dramatic narrative. The elements of the traditional scene are:

- Two or more characters
- The back story: their relationship before the scene
- Conflict or tension between them
- A place
- Dialogue—what is or is not said
- Physical action—what they do or do not do
- The narrator who tells the story from an omniscient, godlike point of view; or from the first-person point of view

The story grows in a sequence of scenes in which characters confront each other—act and react, speak and respond. Each scene develops the story as the characters are changed by the relationships they have with one another. These dramatic scenes invite readers to observe the actions and reactions of the characters, and then decide what has happened and what its significance is. When the dramatic scene really works readers stop being observers and enter the page, becoming one of the characters. The experience of fiction becomes an experience in living.

I have drafted this scene several times in my head and a few times on paper but I don't look back to those failed drafts. If there is anything worth recovering, it will come back in the writing. Some fiction writers plan carefully, as I do when writing nonfiction, but with fiction I have to know just enough to get the characters walking and talking, then they reveal the story to me. I usually write scenes with a technique I call layering. My first scenes are often sketchy, mostly outlining the action, and then I go over and over them, the way a painter lays down coats of paint on canvas, bringing certain elements up and pushing others into the background as I discover the story.

The Characters and Their Back Story

I have been thinking about Blair Morison, a grandfather who retired to care for his wife during her long dying. He retired to his grandfather's house in New Hampshire, where he has begun to a achieve a life with a careful balance, the life of art he had rejected for business. He had even begun a relationship of carefully calculated distances with Sarah Wilson, a woman who had left an abusive husband after her children had grown.

I am influenced by William Gibson, the novelist and playwright who wrote in his study of Shakespeare's plays, *Shakespeare's Game*, "A play begins when a world in some state of equipoise, always uneasy, is broken into by a happening. Since it is not equipoise we have paid to see, but the loosing and binding of an evening's disorder, the sooner the happening the better . . . "

The Happening

Tedd Morison, Blair's thirteen-year-old grandson from Arizona, is being sent to spend the summer with his grandfather. I don't know the reason. I have imagined it is to comfort his grandfather who doesn't want comfort, perhaps because of a divorce, because of the death of his mother, even because his father has gone crazy and killed the rest of the family. I have thought a lot about the child who survives this all-too-frequent family massacre. I don't need to know. Tedd will reveal what has happened when he comes alive on the page.

Blair is at the airport (Boston or Portland, Maine or Manchester, New Hampshire) with Sarah (with Sarah after they have spent a weekend in Boston and made a step closer to commitment?) to meet his grandson whom he hardly remembers.

Narrator and Point of View

I hope the point of view will not be first-person, because this is so hard to write from, but I think it will probably be from the point of view of the grandfather, which will allow his memories, thoughts, and emotions to give texture to the story.

Now you know all I know and I will take you to the airport to meet the plane.

"You're marching."

Blair Morison broke stride and slowed until Sarah Wilson caught up with him. "Sorry."

"The war's over."

"I guess it is. As over as it will ever be." Almost fifty years and still marching. "I look old but feel young. Guess that's good."

"It's good." Sarah took his hand, knowing it would make this old Yankee feel uncomfortable, but when she squeezed he squeezed back. "Don't worry. Tedd's visit will be good for him."

"And for me?" A thirteen-year-old grandson sent uninvited for the summer. Got to be a reason.

This line popped into my head and in using it I dive right into the action. It also prepares the reader for the fact that Blair is a veteran.

It also establishes a relationship—and tension between Blair and Sarah.

And, of course, the war isn't over for him.

This is a sexual relationship but probably a new one. She teases and comforts him.

Someone is coming to visit who will upset the balance of their lives.

Later I will flesh out the scene, but I prefer to emphasize through dialogue the dramatic relationship between the characters that will drive the story forward.

Divorce. Separation. Comfort the lonely old widower who they don't know isn't so lonely? Christ, they could have asked him. Just because he was retired, they can't dump the kid on him.

The reader—and in this case, the writer—learn the back story as we need to know it. The scene doesn't start with a lot of background information before the reader can understand its significance. Beginning writers often deliver too much background too early.

"You're marching again."

Blair turned to snap at her. She didn't own him yet, but she was laughing. "Scared of a teen-ager?"

"Scared of all teen-agers. He probably missed the plane. Overslept. Forgot."

His stereotype of the grandson he doesn't know.

"At least you're on time, that'll show him."

"I'm not on time. I'm half an hour early and you know it. But it was a good weekend. It's been a long time. And Martha? Well, it never . . ."

Blair's way of controlling his life is revealed.

His dead wife enters the scene.

"Don't say it."

"I will say it. She was a good woman and she loved me but she didn't know how to have fun. Hell, I still don't. It wasn't her, it was us."

Back story and new story interwoven.

"Enough. We both have our histories."

"Gramps?"

Blair looked at the gawky kid all knobs and bones that had cut across the concourse.

Surprise. Stereotype broken, Blair off balance, his controlled world already upset.

"Tedd?"

"Yep."

"Your plane doesn't get in until 5:40."

"I got to the airport early. Took the first plane out."

"He's your grandson," Sarah laughed.

"Oh, yes. This is Sarah Winslow. My friend."

"Live-in friend?"

His directness keeps Blair off balance.

"Well, yes, sometimes, I mean . . ."

Tedd grinned and stuck out his hand for Sarah, "I'm used to that."

Hint of the reason he's visiting grandfather.

Blair looked at Sarah but she was getting them all turned around and headed back out to the terminal. He wondered what that meant. Used to what? Sinning? It was all a matter of control, of maintaining the careful balance, the discipline of his days that Sarah invaded from time to time and now Tedd.

Sarah starts playing a controlling role.

"Have you eaten?" he asked Tedd.

"Yep." Tedd answered as he heaved his duffle up on his shoulder, wobbled then got his balance.

"Hungry?" Sarah asked.

Sarah knows the question to ask, Blair doesn't.

"Yep." Tedd grinned and Blair knew it was two against one now. The loneliness he'd worked so hard to cultivate was slipping away. "We'll eat on the drive home."

Am I telling—intruding—when I don't need to? Probably. I'll probably cut this.

"Is it a big farm?"

"No farm at all. A big house on a hill and museum."

Blair's grandfather's museum, Blair used to visit at Tedd's age.

"Of what?"

"War."

New conflict or theme set up. Tedd will be fascinated by the military but Blair is both proud and ashamed of what he had to do in war—and may have to do again.

I have a story—perhaps a novel—to write by building a series of scenes. As the characters interact, I will discover their story. As Joan Didion says, "I don't have a very clear idea of who the characters are until they start talking."

Now that the scene has revealed the conflicts within the story, I can go back like a movie director and change it to explore the conflicts and develop the scene. Some of the elements I can play with include the following.

Point of View

The writer invites the reader to stand at his or her side to view the story. Some writers shift back and forth between points of view as I did in one novel, but that can be very disorienting for the reader.

The scene, as I have written it, is told from an omniscient point of view; the camera is in the ceiling.

> "You're marching."
>
> Blair Morison broke stride and slowed until Sarah Wilson caught up with him. "Sorry."

That wonderful camera can record a character's thoughts, but it is usually a good idea to limit the camera to one character's thoughts.

> Blair Morison broke stride and slowed until Sarah Wilson caught up with him. "Sorry." He thought he had been discharged from his war, half a century before, but again he was reminded that those who survived the intimacy of infantry war were never on leave.

The camera can also zoom in and see the world through a character's eyes.

> Blair Morison broke stride and slowed until Sarah Wilson caught up with him. He smiled. She marched as well, still the nurse in Korea, he remembered seeing her when he was brought in with his heart attack—she was in command in Emergency and he knew she had served in the military long before she told him.

The story could be told from Sarah's point of view.

> Sarah watched Blair march ahead of her, a young paratrooper in a 65-year-old body and wondered if she wanted another commitment at her age, a grandfather and his teenaged grandson dumped on him for the summer.

It can be told from Tedd's point of view.

> Just like Dad, the old fart is still playing soldier, shoulders back, hands out of pockets, eyes straight ahead, "hup-tuh-tree-foah" the way Dad used to march him around the yard before they took him away.

The scene could even be told from a stranger's point of view.

> She never minded waiting at the airport. There was always a story. That tall, old man, ex-military for sure, and the woman hurrying after him and angry that she had to—not his wife, not that kind of anger and the teenager, probably a grandson, in nonmilitary grunge, bandana on his head, earring, pony-tail, slumping along on a collision course with them.

The writer/director has many points of view from which to choose or combine and I find it helpful to think in terms of where the camera can be placed to best reveal the significance of the scene to the reader.

Person

The second person, *you*, rarely works well because the *you* seems to create a direct relationship between writer and reader, while first or third person allows the reader to become the character. Most stories are told in the third person as the scene is drafted. First person appears easy, but it isn't. The *I* has to become a character separate from the reader and that separate person's knowledge of the story is limited. However, first person does have an immediacy and power and can slide in and out of thought and observation easily.

> I marched down the airport corridor trying to keep the anger out of my step. It was another duty, getting Tedd, the grandson I hadn't seen in years for the summer. I'd raised my family, nursed and buried my wife, just gotten to know Sarah, and now a probably snotty teenager shows up with an earring and a boom box.
>
> "You're marching."
>
> I turn and watch Sarah, not girl friend, woman friend, no, more than friend after this weekend but not yet, well, he'd have to think about that and it probably wouldn't be his decision. She was ex-military too, and comfortable with command.

Narrator

The narrator can be someone outside the story or inside the story, as the examples above indicate; but the role of the narrator can come forward and tell the story to the reader, standing right on stage, as the narrator does in Thorton Wilder's "Our Town."

> This is a war story told fifty years after Blair Morison waited until the last German soldier he would kill moved into his sniper rifle's sight and stopped long enough for Blair to so gently, so softly squeeze the trigger.

Voice

Each story has its own narrative voice, the voice of the storyteller who may be inside or outside of the story. It is the voice that attracts us to the story and makes us believe or not believe it. Voice is the magic that is hard to describe but it is the most important element in the story, the music that supports and holds the story together.

The voice, as I have said earlier, is a combination of the personal voice of the writer and the evolving voice of the draft. It is too early for me to hear the voice of this story clearly but in the tension between the characters in the first draft I hear a voice that is dramatic, that says here is a story worth listening to, that is Yankee, ex-military, over-sixtyish.

The voice of the story might say:

> The three were listening to each other with the care we never give those with whom we are close. When one of them spoke, the others turned their heads, almost cocking them as a terrier does, to make sure they were listening and the talker knew they were listening.

As the story evolves I will have another question of voice to consider: the voice of the characters, their external and internal voices, that must be different from each other and from the voice of the story. The reader should know who is speaking from the voice itself, not from the "he saids" and "she saids," which should be used very sparingly.

Tedd's internal voice might say:

> Tedd watches the tall old man marching down the airport corridor ahead of a woman almost as old as he is. This stinks. Who is she, some social worker or his shack-up? It isn't his grandmother. She's dead. And I had plans for this summer, good plans.

His external voice might be:

"I know you don't want me here and you should know I don't want to be here, so it isn't some stupid Disney movie, right?"

Chronology

The scene can moved back or ahead in time.

> "You're marching."
> He realized he wasn't in the airport and it wasn't summer. He was going down that Christmas card road, the Ardennes forest hung with wet snow, into battle. The gray afternoon light reflected from the snow, the sounds of their marching was muffled, and the rumble in the east was not thunder.

Tense

I can even break out of the simple past tense convention of most fiction and tell the story in the present tense.

> "You're marching."
> Blair Morison breaks stride and slows down until Sarah Wilson catches up with him.

Distance

I can move the camera far back and then zoom in close.

> One head stood out down the long corridor to the planes. Other heads hurried, bobbing up and down; others sauntered; some staggered left and right or kept changing pace, but this one steel gray head, hair cropped close, moved in a straight line, at an even pace. Other people got out of that head's way.
> Up close, the face was in duty mode. It was prepared to meet someone, to fulfil an obligation, to lay down lines from the first moment. It was not a cruel face, but a hard one. Strong eye brows, weathered tempered skin, hawk nose and high cheek bones, strong jaw, straight-line mouth and eyes deep set, hidden from view.

Pace

As the scene develops, the writer/director will speed it up to keep the reader interested, slow it down to make sure the reader understands the importance of what is happening. The following lines move fast, as they should when the scene is being sketched out, but they may rush the reader right past the challenge that is taking place.

> "Gramps?"
>
> Blair looked at the gawky kid all knobs and bones that had cut across the concourse.
>
> "Tedd?"
>
> "Yep."
>
> "Your plane doesn't get in until 5:40."
>
> "I got to the airport early. Took the first plane out."
>
> "He's your grandson," Sarah laughed.

It may be better to slow that down.

> "Gramps?"
>
> Blair looked at the gawky kid all knobs and bones that had cut across the concourse. Keerist, he was the one with the bandana, pony tail, ear ring, clothes too big even for me. "Tedd?"
>
> "Yep."
>
> Blair realized he was glaring and his grandson was smiling. He didn't want to sound like a top sergeant, but he did. "Your plane doesn't get in until 5:40."
>
> Tedd kept smiling, "I took the first pane out. I got to the airport early. I always get places early. Like to reconnoiter, scout the territory."
>
> "And surprise the enemy?"
>
> "That too."
>
> "I am I the enemy?"
>
> His grandson kept smiling that startling mature smile. He was only 13. I have to remember. Then he realized Tedd had spoken. "Perhaps we are both enemies."

Character

As the scene develops, the writer/director may drop a character. Sarah may be too much, their relationship may be too early for her to have gone to the airport, maybe the focus should be the grandfather and grandson. Or another character may wander into the scene. Tedd has brought a friend along. Perhaps the friend is a girl, perhaps Tedd is an old sixteen, not thirteen. The characters will take over a scene—and a story.

Back Story

Some writers spend a long time writing out the back story—what has happened to the characters before they step on stage; what do they need, fear, like, dislike; what have they learned, lost, found. I prefer to let the back story evolve as I meet the characters. Sarah talks about being a nurse in Korea and I see how that shapes her and helps her understand Blair if he goes back to war in the story. Tedd may be arriving for the summer because of a parental trial separation or divorce, because he has gotten into trouble, even because his veteran father has gone crazy and killed everyone in the family except for Tedd, who was supposed be home and killed, but who had sneaked away from home and survived. If the latter happened, then all three principal characters share survival guilt.

Action

The action may change as the scene develops. Tedd may have missed the plane, instead of getting there early. He may announce that he is not going to stay the summer or that he intends to live permanently with his grandfather, he may be drunk or high, or catatonic after the shooting, unable to speak.

Second Story

Grace Paley said, "I know I have a story when I have two stories." We have Tedd's story but we also have Blair and Sarah's story. And potentially we have the war-survival story.

Setting

Of course, there is the setting. Eventually it will be the New Hampshire farm that is a museum of war. At the moment it is the airport that may impinge on the story in many ways. Blair may have traveled a great deal before retirement and he may be nostalgic for the life he led—or relieved he will never have to fly again. I suspect that the airport will stand for the transitory, impersonal extended family life of our time.

> Sarah mentioned how many kids there were traveling alone, teenagers and much younger, children flying alone to serve their time with one parent before being shipped back to another family, neighborhood, school. One girl at the hospital said, after an accident, "all eight of my parents will be mad at me." Gate 22. Orlando, dozens of kids being shipped off alone to visit grandparents and a make believe world created by Disney.

Theme

The theme or meaning of the scene comes from the interaction of the characters and the very meaning of the draft may change, scene by scene.

Genre

In writing the scene, I may realize that my novel is really a short story. I have had a nonfiction article leap across genre lines and become a novel. The scene is a fundamental building block of writing and firm. I might, in writing the scene, decide to do a nonfiction book, interviewing grandparents who have had to raise their grandchildren as a second family.

The scene is not planned but observed. I discover the scene—the characters and their story—as I watch them in my mind's eye and as they appear on the page with language clarifying and distorting what I have seen. I feel like Graham Greene, who said:

> When I construct a scene, I don't describe the hundredth part of what I see; I see the characters scratching their noses, walking about, tilting back in their chairs—even after I've finished writing—so much so that after a while I feel a weariness which does not derive all that much from my effort of imagination but is more like a visual fatigue: My eyes are tired from watching my characters.

I do not want to tell the reader *about* the story but to allow the reader to observe then enter into the story, becoming the characters, living the imaginary life until it becomes another life I have lived. Each scene will resolve one conflict and that resolution will bring a new conflict. Scene by scene, the narrative will reveal itself to me as a writer and, eventually, to the reader.

Live Within the Story

The beginning writer wants to know the rules for writing a short story or a novel, but there are few rules external to the story. The story makes its own rules and they cannot be predicted—or broken. That is the delight and the terror of the form.

Eudora Welty says, "The writer himself studies intensely how to do it while he is in the thick of doing it; then when the particular novel or story is done, he is likely to forget how; he does well to. Each work is new. Mercifully, the question of *how* abides less in the abstract, and less in the past, than in the specific, in the work at hand . . . "

The unwritten story imposes its own demands through its telling. The writer does not so much create as accept, does not so much write as listen, does not so much tell as be told.

"I never know what my stories are about until they are finished, until they choose to reveal themselves," explains Kate Braverman, "I merely feel their power, how they breathe on me. I try not to write them. I prefer the rush of having them write me." Jayne Anne Phillips reports, "Real writers serve their material. They allow it to pass through them and have the opportunity to move beyond the daily limitations of being inside themselves. It's like being led by a whisper." Carolyn Chute says that writing fiction "is sort of like when you've got no electricity and you've gotten up in the middle of the night to find the bathroom, feeling your way along in the dark."

To discover just how productive messy personal narrative can be

1. Pick an experience that changed your life.
2. Write it as fast as you can. Write so fast it is hard to keep up.
3. Stop after a page, 250 words, five minutes at most.
4. Don't read it.
5. Take a new piece of paper or save and go to a new screen and write it again without looking back, without thinking back. Let the draft lead.
6. Stop after a page, 250 words, five minutes at most.
7. Don't read it.
8. Write it again without looking back, without thinking back. Let the draft lead.
9. Stop after a page, 250 words, five minutes at most.
10. Don't read it.
11. Write it again without looking back, without thinking back. Let the draft lead.
12. Stop after a page, 250 words, five minutes at most.
13. Don't read it.
14. Write it again without looking back, without thinking back. Let the draft lead.
15. Think back, then read back, noting what surprised you, what you knew that you didn't know you knew.

Three drafts are essential. Five are better. Your vision of this experience that you have thought about for years should be different from what it has ever been. Writing should have led you to a new understanding—or, at least, a new confusion.

It is important you choose an important experience, one you have been thinking about, consciously and subconsciously, for a long time. It is also important to write with velocity. The speed of writing concentrates the writer's vision, freeing the story from preconception and inhibition and freeing the writing from an obsession with premature correctness. Velocity forces the writer to live within the story.

Some beginners think writers begin to create a story with a theme—and a successful few writers do, especially science fiction writers. Other beginners think writers start with plot, and many do, especially those who write mysteries, thrillers, romances and movie-targeted best sellers. Still other beginners believe writers start with a character, and most do.

Remember Welty. There is no one way, there are many ways. In fact, fiction begins with a combination of these elements. Theme is usually discovered as the drafts tell the writer what they mean, but the writer has a territory, a concern, an itch, a question, a problem to explore in the beginning.

Some writers make detailed outlines or use a movie-writer's story board to lay out the scenes in advance, but even those who do not, usually have a sense of the trail (or trails) ahead. Their maps may be detailed, just a rough sketch, or a vision held in the head, but there is a sense that as the characters interact, scene by scene, they will be changed. John Irving says:

> A novel is a piece of architecture. It's not random wallowings or confessional diaries. It's a building—it has to have walls and floors and the bathrooms have to work . . . I believe you have constructive accidents en route through a novel only because you have mapped a clear way. If you have confidence that you have a clear direction to take, you always have confidence to explore other ways, if they prove to be mere digressions, you'll recognize that and make the necessary revisions. The more you know about a book, the freer you can be to fool around . . . I know everything that was going to happen, in advance . . . I have last chapters in my mind before I see first chapters . . . I love plot, and how can you plot a novel if you don't know the ending first? How do you know how to introduce a character if you don't know how he ends up? You might say I back into a novel. All the important discoveries—at the end of the book—these are the things I have to know before I know where to begin.

It is hard, however, for beginning writers to plot. They have read other people's plots. They have not constructed a long fictional narrative. They do not know the territory. Most beginning writers should begin with a character who confronts other characters.

This is the way most writers enter their stories, and even those who plot and plan admit the story begins when a character comes alive and takes control of the story. The writer may have written detailed biographies of the main characters, developed their back stories—what has shaped them before the opening page—but as the characters interact, it becomes their story. Chinua Achebe explains:

> I think I can say that the general idea is the first, followed almost immediately by the major characters. We live in a sea of general ideas, so that's not a novel, since there are so many general ideas. But the moment a particular idea is linked to a character, it's like an engine moves it. Then you have a novel underway . . . Once a novel gets going and I know it is viable, I don't then worry about plot or themes. These things will come in almost automatically because the characters are now pulling the story. At some point it seems as if you are not as much in command, in control, of events as you thought you were.

John Cheever comes down firmly on both sides of the issue: "I never know where my characters come from or where they are going," and "The legend that characters run away from their authors—taking up drugs, having sex operations and becoming president—implies that the writer is a fool with no knowledge or mastery of his craft."

What is certainly true is that the story doesn't wait long to take control. Joan Didion explains, "What's so hard about the first sentence is that you're stuck with it. Everything else is going to flow out of that sentence. And by the time you've laid down the first *two* sentences, your options are all gone." Another time, she writes: "It tells you. You don't tell it."

Elie Wiesel agrees with Didion: "With novels it's the first line that's important. If I have that the novel comes easily. The first line determines the form of the whole novel."

I once sat in a workshop with short-story writer Becky Rule, both a magnificent writer and an extraordinary teacher of writing. She is coauthor with Susan Wheeler of *Creating the Story*. Rule demonstrated how, as soon as she wrote the first sentence, strict rules were established for a particular story. Her first sentence, a typical Becky Rule beginning, was: "When I mention small potatoes, I am certainly not referring to my opponent's manly parts."

Here are the rules she had to follow after writing that first sentence

- The story will be written in the first person.
- It will be written in the present tense.
- The word *certainly* establishes the fact the narrator has an edge.
- The speaker is a female: "his manly parts."
- She is in a conflict, probably political: "my opponent."
- She has an edge but she is not a person brought up to speak rudely, her edge is tempered by what people have expected of her, and that inner conflict between her natural honesty and her sense of propriety is established by the wonderful phrase, "manly parts."
- She has a strong, individual rural New England voice. Her voice sets the music of the story.
- The conflict with her opponent established in the first sentence will be resolved by the last.

All that in just the first line!

Andre Gide said, "The bad novelist constructs his characters; he directs them and makes them speak. The true novelist listens to them and watches them act; he hears their voices even before he knows them." And Gide also knew the importance of getting into the writing any way you can: "Too often I wait for the sentence to finish taking shape in my mind before setting it down. It is better to seize it by the end that first offers itself, head and foot, though not knowing the rest, then pull: the rest will follow along."

The inexperienced writer looks primarily outside the evolving drafts for instruction. The beginning writer looks for rules, principles, theories, lessons, traditions, models. The experienced writer looks primarily inside the text. The writer enters into a world, describes that world and those who inhabit it, discovering the story—and its rules—by writing.

When I write fiction my characters reveal themselves as a photograph does in developer. What is first a pale shadow slowly changes into a sharp-edged portrait. It takes time for us to get to know the people in our lives and it takes layer after layer of writing to make a character come clear. Elizabeth Bowen explains, "The term 'creation of character' . . . is misleading. Characters pre-exist. They are *found.* They reveal themselves slowly to the novelist's perception—as might fellow-travelers seated opposite one in a very dimly lit railway carriage."

While following your characters as they act out their story you need to forget all that you know of writing, all that you have read, all that you have written, just observe and report. Later you will go back over the story, scene by scene, developing your strengths, clarifying, shaping, pacing, and cutting. What do you cut? Follow Kurt Vonnegut's counsel, "Don't put anything in a story that does not reveal character or advance the action."

As you write, you will find yourself going into the story the way the artist steps into the evolving world on the canvas, and then stepping back to see it with a reader's eyes the way the artist steps back in the studio to see the painting whole.

Take a running jump and land in the world of story. You will learn to write fiction by writing fiction. Once you are within the story, the world around you will become clear. You will discover the rules that will govern this particular story. And when you write the next story, the rules will change.

As long as you live and write, each story will be new. You will not know how to tell it until you enter into the telling. You will always have the blessing, as I have in my seventies, of being a beginning writer.

5

Trying on Poetry

Experiencing Poetry

Writing poetry is profound fun, a serious game played with a light touch. If there is a hierarchy of genre, then poetry must be at the peak. Poetry says more with fewer words. Poetry is the bouillon cube of literature; meaning is compressed so that it will boil up in the reader's mind when it is read. Poetry captures the essence of meaning. As Archibald Macleish said in the last lines of his poem *Ars Poetica*:

> A poem should not mean
> But be.

There is no game I play that is as much fun as the writing of a poem. It goes directly to experience, to thought, to feeling. It teaches me as a writer, more than any genre, what is important within the territory being explored. I write about the terror of war and find a poem recounting the discomforting joys of combat. I start to write about the sounds of war—shellfire, machine guns, mines, mortars, grenades, bombing and strafing planes, flame throwers—and discover the more terrifying silence of war.

SILENCE IN WARTIME

After shellfire hail
gravel and bone
silence

After booby trap
surprise
silence

After the patient sniper fires
silence

After the quick strafing
planes make their final pass
silence

After the wounded
"OmyGodOmyGod"
are taken
silence

After dying
black mouths
stuffed with
silence

If the reader is not familiar with contemporary poetry, I can hear some questions that must be answered immediately.

How Come Your Lines Don't Rhyme?

Rhymed poetry isn't written very often these days. Much of the poetry taught in school is rhymed, and it is delightful, but it was written in another time. Rhyme is great fun—I am old enough to have been trained to write traditional poetry—but the danger is that in reaching for a word that rhymes, you pick a word that distorts the meaning, and form comes before content. In contemporary poetry, form should follow meaning. The lines break in a way that clarifies meaning. The classic, formal structures of poetry rarely fit the experience of contemporary life that are explored in today's poetry.

Where's the Meter?

There is a music to my written language, but I do not follow any proscribed meter or beat. I write out loud and tune lines and words to my evolving meaning. I work within the poem the same way I write within the story.

The music, the beat of my poem about wartime silence is purposefully flat. That voice and beat, I hope, allows the terror of what is being said to come through. It is similar to a report a platoon leader might make to his company commander at the end of battle.

In another sense, it is a "silent" poem, saying little on purpose. It is trying to create—in the reader's mind—an enormous silence.

Does Your Verse Have a Pattern?

The stanza breaks merely signal another topic leading up to the wounded and the dead at the end. Some stanzas have three lines, one has two, others four. I used the number of lines I needed to contain my meaning.

In contemporary poetry, we talk of organic form, the form that arises from meaning. I want to focus on each kind of silence, ranging from the silence that comes from each weapon until we come to the silence of the wounded that I hope to make stronger by the "OmygodOmygod." I write about silence and the wounded speak. I think it works. In other words, I think it contributes to the silence of the poem.

Today's poets may write in sonnets, even sestinas, if the form is appropriate to the meaning, but meaning comes first. As Ernest Hemingway said, "Prose is architecture not interior decoration." This statement is even more true of poetry.

What About Punctuation?

Usually I use punctuation, but in this poem I felt the line breaks gave the poem punctuation and the lack of formal marks of punctuation increased the silence created by the poem.

Of course, I was not thinking of these issues when I was allowing the poem to tell me how it wanted to be made. I was looking at the battlefields on which I fought half a century ago. I was listening to the silence of the battlefield and to the poem, trying to get out of its way and allow it to tell itself. In the editing I can rationalize the lack of punctuation, but in the writing, I was just peeling down to the essence of the poem.

The Language Seems Ordinary, Not "Poetic"

Poetic licenses are no longer issued. We do not write poetry in "poetic" language, words and phrases that only appear in poems. Poetry is written with ordinary language, words and phrases that call attention to the subject instead of to themselves.

Poems are not written with adjectives and adverbs, but nouns and verbs. My poem depends on the success of one verb: *stuffed.*

What Are the Rules of Writing?

Each poem, like each story, establishes its own rules. Some of the "rules" I had to follow that came from within the poem:

- I would have to try and make the reader hear an unexpected and loud silence.
- The silence would take place within the noise of combat.
- Each stanza would start with *after* and end with *silence.*
- Most lines would be short since the actions of the weapons on the battlefield are quick, violent, destructive.
- The poem would be short. There would be a great deal of space—silence—around it.

Each poem imposes its own discipline. I could break any of those rules, and I did in the drafts if the breaking of the rule clarified the meaning. The sniper line was long because it implied long patience; the strafing plane line was long because the plane swept from horizon to horizon.

There is magic in writing poetry, but the magician knows how to receive magic and what to do with it. So does the poet. The making of the silence poem removes much of the mystery of writing poetry.

The poem on the silences in war started with a mental note whose origin I do not know. Much of my language is unpoetic and I am prepared for rather ordinary notes that may become poems. Here is all I had in my daybook: *The Silence of War.* That was all I had at first. I didn't know it was a title. It was a line, a fragment of language that contains an intriguing tension: War is loud noise but there is also silence. Why?

Later I made a few notes on my laptop, printed them out the next day and pasted them in my daybook.

> The theater fills with the sounds of war but I remember the silences.
> After shelling
> On patrol
> of the dead

Later I added this handscript:

after the shelling, the pressure of silence
  pushing down
after the cries for medic, ma,
  the open mouths

The mouths surprised me. Later that day I sat at the front of the supermarket waiting for Minnie Mae, took out a 3" x 5" card and wrote:

  remember
  dream
when I think of war
I hear the silence

after shelling

when the cries of the wounded
have been carried to the rear

and the dying have ~~finished~~ done
their duty
and are quiet

the quiet after the Messerschmidt
has flown across the ridge

and the bombs have made no more
noise

the quiet before the attack
when we breathe
to some shallow heart

This doesn't make much sense to me, but that's not important. It is important for those who do not yet write poetry to see the bad writing that may produce good writing. Something is working. I will type and retype it on the computer to see if it works towards its own meaning. I did that, drafting several versions of the poem, just running through it when I had a few minutes with a scrap of paper, my daybook, or a blank screen in front of me. The poem grew to describe a number of kinds of silences and I was determined to make the poem describe a return to battle in the last stanza.

I write more drafts in the doodly moments of life while I am waiting for someone, when I mute the commercials on TV, when I am between appointments or jobs. Usually I mark up the poem, then copy it over or just start it anew. I add—developing—and take away—cutting—at the same time.

Next I wanted to see what I could take away from the poem that would make it stronger. Less can indeed be more. Some poems have to be built up, others cut. Since this is a poem about silence, I wanted to do as much with as little as I could. There should be a great deal of space around the poem. So I cut a number of times before I got to what I thought was my final version.

One of my test readers, Chip Scanlan, thought I lost the poem. He liked a previous draft of the poem but he said he would end it with the breathing and drop the last silence. I understood what he was saying but decided to go with my version. There is no right or wrong, not even what works or needs work, it is just what feels right to the poet.

Then I "published" the poem in my poetry group. I felt pretty good about the poem, imagined there would be praise and some tinkering. I passed out copies, then read the poem. There was an appropriate silence for rereading. After I had read aloud, I found myself marking some changes in the text.

I wasn't sure about those changes, but when I read before an audience I hear the poem differently. Then someone in the poetry group suggested I eliminate the word silence, that the silence was greater without that word. Others seemed to agree. The idea excited me. I had never thought of that. Someone suggested a stronger word than *surprise* but didn't suggest what the word would be. I'd think about that. Someone else said it should be *silences*—plural—in the title. I silently rejected that. Some suggested cutting "OmygodOmygod" but others defended it. Some one questioned the spelling of *strafing*. He was right. It should be with one *f*. The group debated words other than *silence* but didn't come up with one. There was a discussion of whether or not *silence* could be cut at the end and most seemed to feel it had to be there; one felt strongly the poem should end "stuffed with." Another person said it was more than silence, an emptiness, a nothingness and another member said she had thought of silence before the attack but never after battle. All this was stimulating to me. Readers I respected had not just given me compliments but had taken my work seriously, which is the greatest praise.

The next morning I was eager to get to the poem—to continue play. Before I started, I checked my e-mail and another member of the group wrote me that he thought the poem should be the last one in the book manuscript of war poems I'm thinking of submitting and I liked that idea. I played with the poem some more.

SILENCE IN WARTIME

After shellfire hail
gravel and bone

After booby trap
flash

After the patient sniper
fires

After the quick strafing planes

After the wounded
"OmyGodOmyGod"

After dying
black mouths open
silent

I hated to give up "stuffed with silence" but I think the poem is stronger. I'd let it rest and share it with a few readers I trust. Don Graves called. He didn't like *silent*. He wanted *silence*. I think *silence* is too general. Perhaps my poetry-group colleague was right. It could end without *silence* or *silent*. This was not rejection but opportunity, not failure but craft. I might even send the poem off without knowing if it is finished. As Paul Valéry said, "A poem is never finished, only abandoned."

Writing Your First Poem

The best way to enter the game of poetry is to play. Let's write a poem. Forget about rhyme or meter. The poem should grow organically from the meaning. Forget about sentences. Contemporary poems are written in lines, not sentences. We'll talk about the poetic line and line breaks in detail later.

Just list what you think about when you're not thinking—driving in the car, waiting, staring out the window, during the TV commercials, walking or jogging. Be specific. The list may be short or long and the items on the list may be quite ordinary.

I'm going to make a list, but don't try to imitate mine. Every person's list will be different—and my list will be different each time I write it. If making a list doesn't work, wait a while. Try it again.

pale winter shadows on snow
sun on snow
X's call last night: his temptation
  to kill himself
cold sun
sun without warmth
pale winter sky
Belgium
fifty years ago
German

[Phone call, then e-mail as a result of the phone call, a trip to the bathroom, all the typical things that normally interrupt writing. No matter, pick up the list]

on lone patrol
loneliness of war
remember no names from combat
unknown soldiers
joy of loneliness
in movies bunched together
one grenade
one mortar shell
one mine take all
I've become used to cold

This is talking to myself. I don't know if a reader can understand the private meanings, and it doesn't matter. This is for me.

Now look at your list. What surprises you? In my case it is the pleasure of loneliness at war, the satisfactions, the depending on oneself, the aliveness I feel reentering my days in combat. I expect negative feelings, but not the positive ones.

What connects? In my case, the coldness connects with the loneliness and another surprise, I've become used to the coldness. Denise Levertov explains how a poem may come to her:

> It is a sort of vague feeling that somewhere in the vicinity there is a poem, then no, I don't do anything about it, I wait. If a whole line,

> or phrase, comes into my head, I write it down, but without pushing it unless it immediately leads to another one. If it's an idea, then I don't do anything about it until that idea begins to crystallize into some phrases, some words, a rhythm, because if I try to push that into being by will before the intuition is really at work, then it's going to be a very bad beginning, and perhaps I'm going to lose the poem altogether . . . You can smell the poem before you can see it. Like some animal.

I can smell or sense more kinds of coldness than the meteorological kind in my list. I think there may be a poem in the vicinity. I remember talking with my morning walking companion, sculptor Michael McConnell, this morning about the coldness I had to have to let my parents and a daughter die. There's a strange, uncomfortable pride and shame in that. Something is perking.

You may be able just to select specifics from your list and re-order them into the draft of a poem. I'm going to have to play with what the list has stirred up. I am a bit concerned that the poem is taking me back to combat. I feel that I write too many poems about war, but each of us has our personal themes—the central mysteries of our lives that we obsessively return to examine. My combat in the Battle of the Bulge in the winter of 1944–1945 is a territory I still need to explore in writing. Pick the one that surprises you the most—or worries you, or keeps rising up—that you need to explore in what may become a poem.

I have grown comfortable with cold
pale winter shadows ~~of black bare trees~~
black skeleton trees
and in the snow mist
my German soldiers in ambush

we were boys ~~together~~
~~in uniform playing "Bang-bang~~
~~you're dead"~~

we were boys in uniform
playing "Bang-bang you're dead"
in the snow of the Ardennes

I won but they do not stay
in their soldier graves
line each hospital corridor
when I kill father with a nod

give mother the gift of death
let my daughter go

accept the seeping cold
of duty

This isn't a poem yet but it is taking me where I do not expect to go and I still have the loneliness in war and my pleasure in that loneliness to explore in poetry.

Follow in your poem writing what you do not expect to write, being specific, breaking the lines in a way that makes your meaning clear, listening to the music of the poem, discovering the rules within the evolving drafts that will lead you toward meaning.

"No Ideas but in Things"

This statement by the poet-physician William Carlos Williams is one of the fundamental statements of modern poetry. He instructed generations of poets to celebrate the ordinary, the obvious, the things that surround us that spark memories, and imaginings.

After my father died I found a pair of his bifocals in a drawer and in those neatly folded rimless glasses I found a series of poems that I rewrote eighty-eight times, discovering in each revision a way of seeing the world through his glasses, and in doing that I found how to both mourn and celebrate our complex relationship.

Most beginning poets, however, ignore the bifocals and attempt to record the emotions of the moment, thinking that poetry resides in the general and the abstract.

Ah death, the eternal silence,
that leaves unspoken
what might have been said
if one had spoken and the other
heard

The problem with those lines is not only that they they are a badly written generality but that the poet tries to instruct the reader to feel the poet's emotions when, instead, the poet should try to reproduce the moment which caused the poet to have feelings. If the poet recreates the moment, the reader will have his or her own reaction. In the moment recaptured, readers will be transported to their own life, experiencing their own thoughts and emotions. Without looking back at those poems written years ago I see those glasses again.

Each night I stood waiting
as Father added up the day's sales,
then he gave me his salesman's smile
but I could not read his eyes.
I only saw myself in these rimless glasses
and now I know he only saw himself
in my glasses, both waiting for the other
to speak.

In those glasses I rediscover how we were hidden from each other and hear all that we could never say. Just an ordinary pair of glasses left in a bureau drawer, waiting to be found by his only son after the last trip to the hospital.

We're not displaying great poetry here in either case but we are showing the difference between stating emotion and attempting to inspire emotion. The most effective poetry reveals the ordinary in such a way that readers are not told how to think or feel, what to think or feel, but are catapulted into their own thoughts and feelings.

Poetic material is not found in the ozone but under our feet, in the dayliness of our living. Think back to a moment in your life and try to get it down as accurately as you can. Once I thought back to school and saw myself placed, as I always was, in the back row because I was tall and many kids could not see over me. I put myself into that classroom, into that seat and wrote of the most ordinary things:

BACK ROW, SIXTH GRADE

It is always October.
I trudge to school,
kick a stone, leap the crack
that goes to China,
take my seat in the back row, jam
my knees under the desk,
avoiding chewing gum, waiting
for recess. The substitute
teacher hesitates
by the door. The bell
rings. She commands
attention to the text.
I cannot find my place.

There is no meaning
in the words. Nearsighted,
I squint at the blackboard:
the tails of dogs, a banana,
a winding river, a diving
hawk. I am in the wrong grade,
in a foreign school, another
century. I stare out the window,
learn how a robin drives a squirrel
from her nest, imagine
a fear of wings. Teacher
calls my name. I speak,
as surprised as if a bee
flew from my mouth.

Now you know—and I know better than I had known before I wrote the poem—what it was like to be a tall, nearsighted kid who did not yet have glasses, sitting in the back row grade after grade in the Massachusetts Fields School.

That is a poem about education, underachieving students, about students with a case of attention deficit disorder, about day dreaming, about a shy student who didn't speak and therefore wasn't called on, about vision deprivation, about educational theory, educational psychology and a lot of other things, but what appears on the page are William Carlos Williams' "things." List the objects in the room around you.

grandma's backscratcher
lamp I had in high school
hourglass from Holland
computer
Fax
Copier
pictures Norwegian Arctic
Sienna
sign "nulla dies sine linea"
picture of World War I soldier
huge portrait of Holbein
open dictionary

I hope you had better luck than I did with my list. I didn't find any poems lying around my office this morning. No mysteries. No surprises.

I'll look out the window. Look out your window and list what you see.

snow
disappearing rock wall
pine trees
underground house down the hill
no squirrels
puffs of smoke from underground house
gray sky
gray snow mist

In the snow I begin to see images from the past. List what you remember. Things. Details. Specifics. Not feelings. Not thoughts.

sled
Flexible Flyer
Frozen woolen mittens
Smell of damp wool
taste
belly thumping down Wollaston hill
squashed between Uncle Will's legs
snow forts
iced snow balls
an arcing throw
like hand grenades
guard duty in snow in Ardennes
patrolling winter woods
snow enemies
lone German
we fire
warm in childhood snow fort

We should not expect too much of such a list. It is a private list, first of all, with each meaningful item carrying an enormous burden of personal history. But it is in this ordinary list of snow forts and sledding and warmth within cold are the stories, the essays, the poems that will record the history of our life. Here are some poems of mine that grew from such a list. For example, "lone German/we fire" on the list above gave me the following poem.

MY FIRST TRUE WAR STORY

I volunteered to go alone into the winter
woods, find the British moving south
and report back. My rifle at the ready,

I stumbled north through the dark forests
of the Ardennes, leaving deep foot holes
in the snow to follow home. Listen,

I sought the loneliness of war, enjoyed
the excitement of shadows, the sudden
moving branch, the gentle fluttering down

of snow. I hear with skin, feel with ear,
smell to see, my animal self alive to cold,
the Enfield I took from the dying sergeant

so light in my hands. When I high stepped
through the drift at the forest edge
and found myself exposed in the snow meadow

I did not see the German kneeling down,
but heard the firecracker sounds, saw
the snow flowers rising around me as I

knelt toward him, exploded flowers at his feet.
We did not reload, but drew two long tracks
across the snow, smiling as we passed,

then disappeared from each other into woods
where we were once more alone, boy pilgrims
on mission. I remember that joyful day

when I found the British and walked my tracks
back to our lines, a day alone, the beauty
of snow woods and the lonely satisfaction

of the job done. I hope my German found
his way home, sits in a warm room, looking
at snow, seeing my wave as we passed by.

This poem was written some time ago, and I realize that today I would probably not write such a clear narrative. Not because it was wrong or what I'm doing today is right, just because my craft is taking me down different trails. This poem was a breakthrough for me because it was the first poem in which I admitted the usually secret joyfulness of combat, the glorious, elemental dependence on self. It also expressed the compassion that infantry soldiers often felt for the people trapped in a political system where they were trying to kill each other. I never heard a patriotic word or slogan at the front.

You may not have been at war but you have your poetic material from your own domestic wars. The important thing is to enter into the subject and go as far and deep as you have the courage to go.

The relationship between seeing and writing is extremely close. One of the great satisfactions is that we see the world in front of us more clearly than we do if we do not write. And we can see the past. I had this blurred, vague image of a boy—myself—looking at photographs of the first World War and found myself entering a photograph.

MARCHING INTO HISTORY

In the sepia photograph from the book
of the Great War, a boiling cloud sky,
a distant village—steeple and cross,
barns, houses, perhaps a convent and flowing
from the village long stubble fields.
A harvest of shell craters, tipped cannon,
bodies, enemy and friend, bellies swelling,
hiding their belt buckles. Close to the camera
one arm stretches out and the hand is open.
Two fingers gone. At the right of the photograph
a dirt road and a line of Lombardy poplars leading
by the village. On the road, fresh troops marching
to the trenches.

I am a 12-year-old boy lying on my stomach
on the oriental rug where my lead soldiers campaign.
I study the photograph from the Great War. It is 1936.
I will have my father's wish: my own war.
He missed his, sells women's hosiery, does not know,
unblooded, untested, if he is a real man, a true Onward
Christian Soldier. Tonight, if he comes home early,
we will lie in his bed and sing soldier songs,
"Tenting tonight, tenting on the old camp ground,"
"Over there, over there," "It's a long, long way
to Tipperary."

I am 19-years-old when I join the line of soldiers
in the photograph. We are quiet. No songs
just the muffled clatter of guns, mess kits,
grenades, bayonets; the sucking sound
boots lifting up from muck. I feel the heat
from a smoking tank, smell the burnt flesh,
the sweet perfume of decay. The village is larger
than I remember. The fields stretch longer
to the horizon. A horse circles in a field,
dragging a one man plow. The clouds are dark,
still boiling, but it is not thunder we hear.

After the poem was published in the *Boston Globe* on Memorial Day, a good reader and good friend Burgess Doherty wondered if I need the middle stanza. And so now do I. That's the fun of writing, I'll never be quite sure. Read it with; read it without. I will.

Poetry is not contained in great thoughts, distant visions, but in the materials of our individual lives, the specific, resonating details that will reveal the meaning of our lives and will cause others, when they read of our lives, to discover their own.

Play with the Line

The basic tool of poetry is the line.

The line may be empty, a space between lines that sets segments of the poem apart, emphasizes what goes before the space or comes after it, provides a resting space for the reader to remember, think, feel, figure out, connect, imagine.

A line may be one word. Usually it is an important word, such as *silence* was in many of the drafts of the poem earlier in this chapter.

The line may be two words that rub against each other and give off a meaning that is greater than each of the words alone. In the Bible there is a two-line verse, "Jesus wept," that does just that. Fighting Quakers was the nickname of the football team at a pacifist college I visited.

The line may be three words or as many that will fit in one line of type on the page. Long lines create their own kind of music and short lines often are used for emphasis.

Lines are not sentences that complete a thought and are measured by punctuation. In many poems there is no punctuation. The end of the line comes when the poet ends it with a line break.

The line break is central to writing contemporary poetry. The line break is used to shape and communicate meaning. There are few rules about line breaks. In general, they come after an important word, not *the, but, an, a.* But there are exceptions. The rules are the internal rules of the poem itself—what works for the writer and the reader, what makes meaning clear.

If the poet is writing by hand, a change in the line break is usually made with a /. For example:

> I grow comfortable with the cold/ within

On the computer, the poet just starts a new line:

> I grow comfortable with the cold
> within.

Let's go through a poem of mine and I'll show you how to play with the line to discover what the poem says. Remember this is *not* how poets write poems. This is how one apprentice poet wrote one poem.

The poem began with scrawled notes woven through my daybook that I cannot often decipher today. I read "I can not kill this bird" and strange notes that make no sense now but at the time I paid attention, sensing in the way a cat does that there may be a chipmunk in my rock wall, that there may be a poem somewhere in the experience that is drawing away from life but seems to have a destination—a significance not yet expressed. The feeling is like meeting someone and saying, I'd like to know that person better. I pay attention.

More notes and a word I now know is important—*attend*—appeared but it did not seem important at the time. However, if I hadn't been writing—scribbling—with velocity and in ignorance that word would not have fallen accidentally to the page.

The point is that the poet has to receive the line, the word, the image, and the poet has to be receptive to what seems trivial, a cliche, documentably bad writing, because it has led to the clues that may seek each other out and coalesce into something that may become an early draft of a poem. This takes patience and experience, trust that the writing will produce more writing.

In my casual daybook jottings I realize, looking back, that I am looking for lines, breaking off the fragments, leaving lines behind. Some of these breaks are conscious but most are not and many have nothing to do with an eventual poem. Some are there just because I came to the edge of the page and moved down to the next line.

> The squirrel dared my wheel
> and lost

That was a conscious and predictable line break. It imitates the action and emphasizes the loss.

> observe
> I stop and ~~attend~~ his slow dying dance
> in the rear view mirror
> Should I go out to ~~stand~~ (attend)
> his dying
> or backing up, fast?

I'm not even sure now what all of this means but it is interesting that I crossed out the word attend that will be crucial to the final poem and potentially add it later. The poem is telling me how to write it. I may be showing too many drafts, but few poems arrive almost complete; most are worked until they achieve spontaneity.

> ~~We made the~~
> ~~De~~
> Father ordered me to let him go.
> (~~and in that final heart attack~~)
> I executed his command,
> sitting with a doctor
> on a leather couch
> (coming to a decision) signing a paper

This leap to my father's death was a complete surprise. The poem did that on its own. I think that working on lines—fragments—that are far less than sentences encourages such leaps, a kind of wandering inattention to what lies around on the outskirts of what may become a poem.

> Mother's gift was requested over a telephone with nurse
> <—Lee ~~I now forget to~~ Next may the
> kids use my
>
> When it is time
> will they attend
> or

Lee is our daughter, whom we had to let go after her brain waves went flat. The flow of notes reveal I am wondering if my children will attend me. Now I complete the first typed version where I am giving more conscious attention to each line and how it might break to tell me, then a reader, what it means.

The squirrel dared my wheel
and lost.

I stop and attend his slow dying
in the rear view mirror.

Father ordered me to let him go
and I executed his command,
sitting on a leather couch
with a young doctor
chatting.

I killed mother on the phone.
Telling the nurse to let her go,
let her go.

The next morning her bed was stripped
and empty.

My daughter's brain wave was straight,
the tone even even even.

I called the funeral home before she died,
imagined her rising, laughing,
and dream her rising still.

Now you can see how I have used the line to present an image or a thought, and broken the lines for emphasis. I kept playing with the lines and below is the fifth typed version in which I backed off to start the poem earlier. I have reproduced how I have worked (played) with the draft—cutting, adding, ordering to allow the poem to express itself. In all of that I am working with line, generally writing with longer lines that seem appropriate to what I am writing, a poem about the accidental death of a squirrel—which I missed in real life—but killed in the poem.

The poem is very much about that real death of the squirrel. As Flannery O'Connor said about a "metaphorical" wooden leg in her story "Good Country People," it was a real wooden leg. It is the real death of a squirrel; then it may be about other deaths as well. Later I will know more of what this poem is about. I do know that I must write it, that it will be an important poem to me, even more important it will turn out, than I could have imagined, and it all turns on that word I first crossed out, *attend.*

I WILL ATTEND

I follow the tunnel between the trees racing
toward me, listening to Mozart, imagining home,
when a squirrel blurs across the corner of my eye
and I swerve toward the slowing woods.

I did not even feel our meeting through the wheel
but in the rear view mirror I see the squirrel,
run back to attend his dying.

Father had ordered me to let him go and I executed his command,
sitting on a leather couch with a young doctor ~~offering me~~
~~And lawyer form signed~~
~~his lawyer form~~
~~arranged father's release~~,

~~the chance to give the gift of death, signed his paper,~~
~~then~~ took mother home, ~~and~~ drove to New Hampshire
~~to bring~~ brought my family down, playing father, playing son.

He left before I returned.
arguing ~~that~~ with
~~persuading~~
I killed mother on the phone, ~~telling the~~ late night nurse
~~to~~ he should let her go, let her go, hung up, told
~~telling~~ myself
it was what
~~she~~ Mother would have wanted

And when I came to ~~her~~ mother next morning,
I found her bed stripped, the mattress flat,
no memory of her resting there nine days;
eight and one-half nights.

When my daughter's brain wave ran straight,
the monitor tone even even even,
I went to her mother, sisters, boyfriend in the waiting room }?
>?
~~and w~~When the doctor came I nodded,
left to call the funeral home ~~before~~ while she died,
imagined her rising, laughing,
and dream her rising still.

~~When I was done with business,~~
~~Lee was somewhere else~~

I pay no attention to the squeal of brakes,
the wind from passing trucks,
the angry yells.

I will attend this dying
if it takes till night.

Now I know what the poem is about. I arranged my father's death, then went home with Mother and she sent me back to New Hampshire to collect my family. I was not with him when he died, and although he would understand that what I did was right, I feel some guilt about his loneliness at that moment.

Two years later, Mother died alone. I had gone home with my family for the night. Again, she would understand, but part of me feels that I, her only child, should have been with her.

We had to let our daughter go. Each of us said good-bye to her alone, and I went to make arrangements with the funeral home while she was still alive. I did all the things I had to do and Lee would have understood, but I feel guilty about that and in writing this poem, I have "attended" my feelings for the first time. And there is a strange comfort in writing this poem.

In writing the poem, in concentrating on the lines and how they should break, I am dealing with my feelings. There is solace in that in a way I cannot understand. And if the poem is published and shared, readers will bring their own stories to the poem and may construct a poem that is partly mine, partly theirs, bringing comfort to both.

Now I share the poem with my poetry group and make notes on their reactions that lead to more changes. I have some distance on the poem and can go through it and produce a final—for the present—version.

I WILL ATTEND

It could have been a pine branch on the road, a frost crack,
a stone, but in the rear view mirror I see the squirrel,
race back to attend its dying.

I negotiated Father's death, as he wished,
signed the papers while the young doctor talked philosophy,
    took mother home,
drove to New Hampshire, brought my family down, playing
    father, playing son.

But he had left before I returned.

I killed Mother on the phone, arguing with the night nurse:
let her go, let her go. She did not respond
but when I came to sit with Mother next morning,
her bed was stripped,
the mattress flat.

When my daughter's brain wave ran straight,
I waited with her mother, sisters, boyfriend
and when the doctor came I nodded then left
to call the funeral home while she died,
imagined her rising, laughing,
she'd been teasing after all.
I dream her rising still.

I pay no attention to the squeal of brakes,
the wind from passing trucks,
the angry yells.

I will attend this dying
if it takes till night.

What rules there are come from within the poem. Writing produces a living text that can change and grow as its writer and its readers change and grow.

6

After Writing

Create a Writing Community

Writing is a private act with a public result, and most of us need a writing community that both provides companionship in our solitude and a staging area that will ease us into publication before strangers.

The contradictory needs for solitude and community became clear to me when I retired from the university, and I have organized my day to respond to both sides of my nature.

I get up at 5:30 in the morning and meet a few cronies for coffee and walk with them, then retreat to my office, emerging for lunch with Minnie Mae or others, do errands, retreat to my office for an hour or so alone in the late afternoon, spend supper time and the evening with Minnie Mae.

If I spend too much or too little time with others, my day becomes unbalanced. Everyone has to develop his or her own rhythm, but it has to include a period alone if the writing is going to get done.

The Community of Writers

As I reach out to create the writing communities I need, I have one rule: I do not share my writing in process with anyone who does not make me want to write. When I get a response from the members of my writing community, I hurry back to my desk, excited by the problems, the possibilities, the strengths I have discovered. I have work to do and I am eager to get at it.

My test readers may be critical, supportive, obsessed with detail, only interested in the overall effect, concerned with only one genre of the four I practice, but they all make me want to write after they have responded to my draft, or they do not remain in this community I cultivate carefully.

Another test of the members of my community is that they share work with me. I get the most help from those who are writing themselves. They understand the territory, they know the feeling of writing and they know the choices the writer faces within the act of writing.

They choose the form and the amount of the work, it may be frequent or infrequent, but I need to read the work in progress of others to understand and develop my craft. I also want to return the favors I am indebted to have received from them. And when I read and respond to their drafts, I hope I make them as eager to return to their drafts as they make me.

It isn't easy to keep reaching out to develop a writing community. It should be, but it isn't, and I want to be honest about this so that you will understand and ignore the disappointments along the way. Many people in the academic world do not understand sharing. They feel competitive, threatened, uncomfortable when shown a draft by a colleague. They do not know how to respond without criticism.

There are people who say they have read your work, and haven't. Their comments refer to a movie or a TV show on the same subject. Some readers are jealous. They want to write on the same topic and see you as a threat. Some only know how to criticize in a negative, destructive manner. Others will criticize your work but show none of their own. Some will only judge your work on their terms, evaluating it against what they have seen or what they expect you to write, not on your draft's own terms.

I have also found that praise can hurt more than criticism if you are praised for what you did not intend to do. I need a writing community and I do not know how to find one without sharing my writing and making myself vulnerable.

I have learned, and now admit, that I need support from my writing community more than criticism. I can usually tell what doesn't work, what doesn't achieve my dreams, what is flawed, awkward, embarrassing. In fact, I tend to think everything in my draft is terrible; criticize me and I will agree with you. What I don't know is what works for a reader and what, with work, will do the job. I need test readers who tell me my potential strengths so I can develop them.

I've also learned to take command of my test readers and tell them what I need from them.

I know this organization isn't right but do I have something worth saying?

The voice isn't right yet, and I know that, but does the organization work for you?

I know the draft's messy, but do you hear the voice and does it make you trust the piece?

Where does the draft bog down, where do I need to speed it up?

What can I cut?

What don't you understand? What needs to be developed?

Would you stop reading? Why?

With telephone, fax, postal mail and e-mail, my writing community spreads across the country. I will describe my writing communities and what each member contributes as a way of helping you develop writing communities that respond to your needs.

First are the members with whom I share almost everything I write and with whom I am in almost daily contact in person, by phone, fax, or mail: stamped or computer sent.

Minnie Mae has supported me in every way, telling me my work is worthwhile when I lose faith, reminding me it isn't so damned important when my faith inflates, getting angry at those who attack me when I need defense, reading copy with a critical eye, and always making sure what I say makes sense and is clear. Hemingway said that every writer needs a "shit detector." Minnie Mae is my shit detector.

I met Chip Scanlan when I was writing coach to the *Providence Journal*, and his insightful questions and critical comments revealed he cared about writing as I do. We have been in almost daily touch as his career took him from Rhode Island to Florida to Washington, D.C., and back to Florida, where he is writing director at the Poynter Institute in St. Petersburg.

He is the only person I regularly talk to about a draft before writing it—a very hazardous activity—and to whom I show early drafts—also dangerous. He understands the whole range of the writer's life from the emotional and intellectual world that surrounds the line to the difference a comma makes. No one could have a closer and more helpful friend. His presence is always felt when I am writing, supposedly alone.

Don Graves is a writer and student of teaching writing whom I talk to almost every day, often more than once a day. Recently, in dedicating his latest book to me, he made the point that I have influenced him although I had "not read any part of this book." We share poems in draft by fax but not many other drafts these days, yet he is a major contributor to my writing community, and our relationship reveals there are many ways in which members of a writing community help a writer.

Elizabeth Cooke is a novelist who lives in northern Maine where she teaches writing. She was a former graduate student who disappeared from my life, then appeared again. We worked together on a special graduate course in which we shared our writing, responding to each other's work in an organized manner. When the course ended we had established a professional relationship we did not want to end. We continue to share, and her perceptive eye always improves my drafts. She is able to enter into my world and my voice and ask questions that are often tough but always kind. She also is a reader who understands what I am trying to do. And when she gets it, it is got; I can go on with confidence.

There are many others—from New Hampshire to Idaho and back—as I share both specific drafts and the shoptalk that enriches this writing community that is so important to those of us who spend hours alone at our desks.

Many beginning writers find it valuable to join formal writing communities that meet regularly to share their work. I have joined and left many writing groups over the years.

The reasons I have left include an unhealthy competition, members who attack others but who do not share their own work, members who take themselves too seriously but their work not seriously enough, groups that confuse destructive criticism with high standards, and, most of all, groups that make me avoid writing and rewriting when I leave.

For years now, I have been a member of a poetry group that makes me write poetry, provides constructive criticism that reveals what works as much as what doesn't work, produces a grand diversity of responses, shares delight in our craft, and makes me want to write when I leave. We meet in the evening of the second and fourth Thursdays of the month. We go to a different member's house each time and start at seven and end at nine. First, we pass around printed copies of our poems. The host reads aloud first. People respond. The writer says, "thank you" when he or she has received enough response and the person on his or her left then reads. We have thirteen members at the moment and because so many are busy we have five to eight at a meeting.

The group is important to me because

1. I produce many poems that I would not have written. I *must* have a poem for each meeting—no excuses—and so I do.

2. I find out what works. I can usually tell what's wrong with a poem, but I don't know what works. The group often finds strengths of which I was unaware or unsure of that I can develop.
3. The group spots errors I overlooked.
4. I enjoy and need the sense of community, the time out of the week taken to share poetry that is made by people who take their craft, but not themselves, seriously. And I am inspired by the different ways we view and celebrate the lives we are living through poems of gloriously different styles and voices.

What follows is a case history of a recent poem and how my writing communties helped me.

THE MILL OWNER IN THE MAHOGANY FRAME

In 1928 grandfather's shadow
escaped his mahogany frame,
slid down the wall, crept
across the oriental rug
where I played.

It was as heavy as the bearskin robe
in Uncle Will's touring car.
Heavier.

This morning
I trim my beard
to grandfather's photograph.

Last night in bed I turned
from the one I love,
curled under his heavy shadow.

Today I drive by the Newmarket Mill
see the children inside
the women at the looms

A man at an office window
his arms crossed
wearing our beard

In papers folded under horse hair
comforters in a steamer trunk
from Scotland

I find he was not always
the mill owner,
the deacon

But first a bookseller
in Glasgow

A poet
a dreamer
a widower when the church
arranged marriage to Grandma
an Islay spinster

Then he became a mill owner
in a new world

He lived in grand house
with a circular drive
a Newfoundland dog
Irish maids

Grandma kept him
in his mill owner photograph
on the wall of each rented flat
after the mill failed

Grandfather left the photograph
to work as bookkeeper
in Philadelphia

Paper cuffs protect
his shirt sleeves
but ink stains his hand

Grandma baked bread
to sell in Dorchester
brought up the children
the grandchildren
under the photograph
in the mahogany frame

My writing community extends across the country and when I completed an early draft of a poem about a grandfather that I thought was close to a final draft, at least good enough to publish in my poetry group, I mailed a copy to Elizabeth Cooke. A few days later she called in the evening and I grabbed my daybook where I had pasted that draft of the poem.

First of all, she gave me encouragement. Perhaps there is a poem there, she implied, something worth pursuing, exploring toward an understanding. As we talked I remembered my saying that there may be two poems here and Elizabeth, laughing, saying, "two books?"

She told me the places that surprised her, the lines she thought worked, and I put check marks by them. Some of the things she mentioned were:

- Elizabeth liked the unexpectedness of mill owner and mahogany. I hoped she felt an interesting tension: He was "framed," pun intended.
- She had problems with *crept* and she used *slide* instead of *slid*; I marked it to look at it again to see if the poem was saying what it meant to say. She mentioned the weight of *crept* and couldn't understand why I had given it that power.
- She mispronounced *Islay* which should be "Eye-luh" and I wondered if I should change the real name to one that gives the reader no problem.
- Elizabeth wondered why I shifted into present tense. I had no idea but in the next draft I went to present tense to see if it brought an immediacy to the poem.

It may not look as if Elizabeth did very much but she had taken the poem seriously, not rewritten it but opened it to my renewed vision. A reader can't do much more than that.

I had made myself vulnerable and I had not been attacked but helped. I had been told what worked for her and then what needed work in her opinion. I let the poem lie fallow overnight but the next day I started through it line by line, seeing it anew. I wasn't making her corrections, I was not seeing the poem with her eyes but my own eyes, going more deeply into the poem, liberated in some way I do not fully understand by her reading.

I found myself writing long lines, cutting, shaping, as the poem told me what it had to say and how it might be said. It was ready to be shared by my poetry group. Some of their reactions to the draft I shared:

- The group seemed to think there was a poem here but there was a great deal of discussion of the first verse. One person suggested cutting *on me* and another said it could not be cut. People were confused by all the people but then they realized if they were all cut, the reader would not know the terrifying power of the shadow, the burden of living up to the standard of the mill owner who turns out not to have been a mill owner most of his life. The discussion was detailed and helpful because it forced me to reconsider each line and the impact of the whole verse.

- Several people did not understand the term *extraordinary means* and therefore did not make sense of the line that refers to mill-owner coldness that made it possible to decide to let my father, mother, daughter die.
- One person needed more about the attic, the papers from the trunk, for example, that were in an early draft. I can certainly fix it. This part of the poem, unlike my mother and the uncles, is not autobiographical.

The group seemed to like the ending and so the next morning I went to work again, trying to enter the poem and follow its lead. In the days ahead I revised the poem again and again, reassured by my readers that I had a poem worth working on and stimulated by the different ways they saw the same piece of writing. At the moment this is the poem, but as I read it I wonder if . . .

THE MILL OWNER ESCAPES HIS MAHOGANY FRAME

At Sunday dinner, I study the brown photograph
of the Grandfather with my name. I cannot find
myself in that righteous face.

Mill owner, deacon, man of means, he lived
in a house high on a hill I have never seen
but as I watch, his shadow escapes the mahogany frame,
falls across Mother, Father, the uncles
who never measured up.

I shove back my chair, run from the mill.
I will weave poems on my loom
but when I grow a beard it is grandfather's.

He is the one, last night in bed,
who turns from the one I love, the soldier
who pulls the bayonet out and moves on,
the young husband who divorces his first wife,
pays his bills on time, does not loan money to friends,
signs the order to let father, mother, daughter die.

This morning, looking for an old coat in the attic,
I remember Grandfather's funeral trunk
Mother let me open.

A Black Watch shawl, a packet of brown edged papers
tied with a string. I cut the knot, unfold each page,
read the old fashioned hand.

Grandfather is not a mill owner.

After his photograph was taken he loses the mill,
the house high on the hill, and leaves the photograph
to work as bookkeeper in Philadelphia where he dies
twelve years before I was born.

Paper cuffs protect his shirt sleeves
but ink stains his hand,
the poems written after the accounts are done.

The Community of Editors

If you keep writing and submitting your manuscripts to publishers, editors will join your community. When I first started writing, I fell into a male attack/counterattack mode. I had submitted draft. The editor attacked the draft. I counterattacked. It was personal combat. Of course, the editor won.

To become a writer, you have to develop your own vision of the world and your own language with which you capture and communicate your world. It took me years to realize the best editors want the same thing: to make you even more of what you are, to cultivate your individuality.

I had to learn to make use of the editing that taught me the traditions of each genre in which I published and then to take advantage of those editors who could encourage my difference that extended the horizons of the tradition. The more experienced a writer I became, the more I began to see editors as collaborators. The published draft is the product of the collaboration between a writer and an editor.

To make this collaboration work, I listen carefully to what the editor is saying—and the more what the editor is saying threatens me, the more emotional I become, the more likely there is something to pay attention to. The editor, after all, is my test reader. If the editor doesn't get it, then readers won't get it.

As I developed as a writer, I realized my ego was not invested in the draft I had submitted as it had been, but that I had developed a greater ego: I had a hundred ways to say anything. If an editor didn't get it, I could try many other ways to say it that would satisfy the editor, the readers, and myself.

When I have a new editor, I greet this person as a collaborator, saying I need editors, that they make me more courageous, more willing to try experiments that may or may not work. I also promise, when I can, to deliver ahead of deadline—my weekly columns are delivered eight days ahead of publication—so there is time for me to respond to the editor's questions and comments myself. I prefer, when possible, to do my own revisions.

I expect to learn from and with my editors and I have, for the most part. The relationship of editor and writer may become as complex as any relationship. It is, after all, a professional marriage. But I enter into it the way I try to enter into any human relationship, with the positive attitude that we will make it work.

The Community of Literature

Of course, the community of writers to which we all belong is enormous. It includes all the writers, living or dead, we read for instruction and inspiration. Here are notes from my daybook that show this writer reading a published writer—Wil Haygood of the *Boston Globe*—for instruction in our craft.

> To write this morning, I read. That is not a normal pattern for me but always helpful when it occurs. Yesterday, reading the *Boston Globe Magazine* I knew I would go to school and the instructor would be Wil Haygood.
>
> I read the lead on his article "The Remarkable Journey of Willie Edward Gary" and then read it aloud to Minnie Mae, later read it again to Chip Scanlan when he called. An article of his is going to be the Fourth of July cover on the *Washington Post Magazine* and he is a fan of Wil's [and my closest friend outside of Minnie Mae and my daughters.] We have often commented on how writing that reaches beyond us is not intimidating as it should be, but inspiring.
>
> Here's Wil's lead:
>
>> They're little nowhere towns—Okeechobee and Sand Cut, Pahokee and Indiantown—snug places in the backwoods of southern Florida. Travel town to town, up and across Route 1—along the migrant road loop—and you'll see figures loping down orange groves, wading into sugar cane fields. Time just seems to peel away. Farmland has long

> demanded a cruel price, no matter what region of the country. Southern Sundays, can unfold like blankets. There's an outdoor church service under way on a streetcorner in Pahokee. The sun's up; the minister's voice is high; the chairs are aluminum. A mere dozen gathered souls looking for strength, convinced the size of their congregation is plenty enough. Mock religion elsewhere, but not here, not in the deep, deep South.

I read the paragraph for its music, finding within it the quality of the best jazz, freedom within discipline, individuality within tradition, familiar notes ordered into surprise. I should not—and could not—imitate Wil but when I write this morning, I should try to allow my voice to solo, to run free within my craft and our tradition, to write with the ease of that paragraph. I don't know or care if it was easy for Wil to write—it is easy to read.

And an irony, the paragraph is just difficult enough, unexpected enough to force my attention.

I am interested in the organization of the article. He tells the story over and over again. Once more a jazz reference that I hope isn't racist. Wil plays the melody he's made familiar to us, embellishing and deepening it each time.

Things I note in that first paragraph:

They're little nowhere towns—	*"nowhere towns"*
Okeechobee and Sand Cut,	
Pahokee and Indiantown—	*impact of specifics*
snug places in the backwoods	
of southern Florida. Travel	*immediacy of "Travel"*
town to town, up and across	
Route 1—along the migrant road	*Foreshadow: "migrant . . . loop"*
loop—and you'll see figures	*"figures" They are not seen, known, but I'll get to know them in the article.*
loping down orange groves,	*"loping" precisely right verb*
wading into sugar cane fields.	*"wading" precisely right verb*
Time just seems to peel away.	*"peel away" Strong image.*
Farmland has long demanded a cruel price, no matter what region of the country.	*puts article in larger context*

Southern Sundays, can unfold like blankets.	*Image: "unfold like blankets"*
There's an outdoor church service under way on a street-corner in Pahokee. The sun's up; the minister's voice is high;	I hear *his voice*
the chairs are aluminum.	I see *the chairs*
A mere dozen gathered souls looking for strength, convinced the size of their congregation is	*"gathered souls" hint of up yonder*
plenty enough. Mock religion elsewhere, but not here, not in the deep, deep South.	*"Mock" Again directly spoken to reader—immediacy*

Of course an autopsy does not recover the person and I can only learn so much from Wil. The rest is mystery, but I can try to move close to the mystery, perceive the craft that precedes art.

Other lines of many in the article that instruct me:

"L. C. just smiled. The smile was as rich as applause."

"The Garys gathered close. Palms touched palms."

" . . . would put her babies in potato sacks next to cane fields. They'd howl; she'd pick."

" 'Day care' was field care."

"They love just to see each other walk up and down the stairs."

" . . . people holding on, people with callouses on their hands . . ."

" . . . from the tape deck of their Rolls-Royce, which just hums along in its own fine silence."

Writing communities grow out of classes, are organized by a community, a church, or an adult learning center. But you can develop your own writing community, by reaching out, sharing drafts, asking writers whose work you like how they wrote it and reading the Wil Haygoods and the Will Shakespeares who instruct us by their solutions to our writing problems.

When we go to our desks to write alone, we are not alone.

The Art of Revision

Rewriting begins before you put the first word on paper and continues until you edit the final draft—which may, in turn, inspire revision.

At first, this may seem discouraging. In school and on the job, revision has been analogous to punishment. Rewriting is seen only as the solution to failure. But revision lies at the center of the writing process, the activity that provides joy, inspiration, surprise, concentration, closure. Revision for yourself, the first reader, and editing for other readers is necessary for effective writing. Listen to what the following writers say about revision.

Katherine Patterson:

I love revision. Where else can spilled milk be turned into ice cream?

Neil Simon:

Rewriting is when playwriting really gets to be fun. In baseball you only get three swings and you're out. In rewriting, you get almost as many swings as you want and you know, sooner or later, you'll hit the ball.

John Kenneth Galbraith:

In my own case there are days when the result is so bad that no fewer than five revisions are required. However, when I'm greatly inspired, only four revisions are needed before, as I've often said, I put in that note of spontaneity which even my meanest critics concede.

Bernard Malamud:

I love the flowers of afterthought.

Revision is too often confused with editing. In rewriting, the focus is on the writer's own reseeing, in exploring and developing the topic so the writer can discover what to say and how to say it. Revision is a private act with an eye cocked toward the reader. In editing, the focus is on the reader, making sure that what the writer has decided to say is clear to the reader. Editing is a public act with attention on the reader, only a glance given to the writer's needs. The revision process takes all the writer knows about the subject and narrows it down to a final draft; the editing process clarifies that draft so that it can be read and understood by many readers.

During revision the writer looks forward from the point of view of the creator who is discovering the evolving meaning; during editing, the writer looks backward from the point of view of the reader.

There are genre differences in revision but they are only matters of emphasis. In poetry and fiction the attention may linger longer with the writer; but if the most "creative" writing is to be read, attention must be paid to the reader, and there must be editing as well as revision. In the corporate memo and the research grant proposal, the writer had better take the time to explore and understand the subject through revision if editing is to make that message clear. Revision is the craft of seeing what you have written, not what you planned, hoped or thought you wrote. Revision is the ability to read your own drafts with the writer's eye, distancing yourself from yourself.

The Revision Attitude

Writing is an experimental act. In the search for meaning, the writer—and the artist, the actor, and the scientist—proceeds by trial and error. I hook one word to another, reach up above the workbench and grab a different word; plug a clause into a sentence, turn it around and try it again; shape a paragraph, taking a little off the end, building up the middle, sharpening the leading edge.

There are many potential right ways and wrong ways to say something, ways that are right or wrong in the evolving context of the draft. The question is what works and what needs work.

Effective writing develops from error—the wrong word allows the writer to hear the right word, the collapse of syntax exposes the possibility of an unexpected meaning, the harsh sound of a poor sentence allows the writer to hear the melody that supports the meaning, the paragraph that runs off the road shows where the road should go.

Attitude controls revision, and the writer should know that failure is necessary, failure is instructive. Only when we fail to say what we imagined we would say do we discover what we should say and how we should say it. We should train ourselves to welcome and make use of instructive failure.

Revision Before Drafting

Meditation tells us to empty our minds and we find that almost impossible. Awake and asleep, talking to others, doing our work, reading, watching TV, driving the car, attending meetings—we carry on continuous interweaving conversations with ourselves. Writers tune in to those conversations: What are we saying to our other selves, what are we saying to others? We surprise ourselves by what we hear.

This morning a breakfast crony asked me why I had made the decision to come to the university when I was thirty-nine. As we drove home I told him the story, but I also heard another story telling itself underneath the oral draft. It would keep surfacing in a word, a phrase, a line.

After I left him off, I found a word that would capture and trigger this story that I needed to tell myself: *discontent.* When I went to my computer I found myself typing in a note that would lead to a future column. It is my habit to put these notes into the format I use to send my columns in to the *Globe*, as the notes may turn into a lead or when typing in the notes I may find myself drafting the first half of the column. Here is today's note:

Sitting on the porch looking back . . .	} Realize a
	} powerful vein
	} of discontent
	} runs through
Computer down, anxious to get to work	} my life

[1st marriage—strain—not to be here but there.]

Discontent has its unhappy aspects for the person feeling it AND the people around them. What are they . . .

BUT
better than content.
{et

I have been revising in my head and on the page, and I will continue to do this naturally, considering and reconsidering the role of discontent in my life and in the lives of others. I brought the topic of discontent up in a conversation with Minnie Mae in the car and in a conversation with Chip Scanlan on the phone. In those conversations I pay as much attention to what I am saying as to what the other person is saying. I may write nothing down or I may capture an idea or a voice on the 3" x 5" cards I carry in my pocket all the time, in my daybook, on the laptop beside my chair in the living room.

Revision During Drafting

As I write, I revise. What I intend to say changes as I say it. Each word predicts the next word, each clause the next clause, each sentence the next sentence, and so on. Writing is revising: the hint, the guess, the suspicion, the intent changed by its language, its audience, its context, its evolving meaning, its amplifying voice.

In drafting I often write in spurts of one to three paragraphs to get started, then in chunks of six to eight paragraphs, going back and reading the chunk of writing to discover what I said rather than what I thought I was saying. Once I know what I have said, I can put it back on track or, more often, follow the track, developing and clarifying what I have found myself saying. As John Fowles says, "Follow the accident, fear the fixed plan—that is the rule." I start to write the column on discontent:

> Driving down the highway, a young friend asks why I made the decision, at the age of 39, to come to the university and, as old men will, I told him more than he probably wanted to know.
>
> Of course I wasn't so much telling him as telling myself in the hope of discovering a meaning or order I had not seen before. ~~Writers,~~ I confess what Minnie Mae knows only too well, that writers talk to listen to themselves. I "write" as I speak, telling a story I do not expect.
>
> At one level it was familiar, the lines worn with use, personal cliches I have told before: "When I was in college I wrote nothing but poetry, never worked on the college newspaper. I wanted to be a great poet but those jobs were taken."
>
> I added a another familiar line, "I also wanted to be a great novelist but those jobs were also taken" and then I added a flourish, "I looked in the want ads. Nothing."
>
> My friend seemed to nod in an encouraging manner. No matter, I would have gone on anyway. "I went to work on a newspaper because I wanted to write poetry, went to *Time* because the newspaper publisher wanted me to be an editor and I wanted to write a novel, freelanced after I was fired by *Time*—they wanted to make me a TV producer—and freelanced magazine articles because I didn't want to write magazine articles."
>
> As my friend got out of my car at his house, I finished the story of my life. "I came to the university to teach journalism because I wanted to write fiction and poetry."
>
> He laughed and I went on telling my story to myself, how I wrote—and continue to write—books on writing and teaching because I want to write fiction and poetry.
>
> As I went down to my office, I felt the familiar old man's guilt that I hadn't done what I should have with my life and I even heard my first wife's voice during a divorce more than forty-five years ago saying that

> I was never content. I wanted to be out of college when I was in college, whatever I was doing I always wanted to be doing something else.
>
> I sat before my computer and waited for the guilt. But it didn't come. I heard the new story that lay under the story I had told my friend. I had lived a life of discontent.

As I wrote this, I kept waiting for the spot where I stopped and revised during the drafting but it didn't come. I have to remind myself that one revision decision is not to revise, to accept the flowing text. I rush on towards the end I don't yet know but can sense just ahead of me, in the last three hunderd or four hundred words.

This is typical. My columns are about eight hundred words long. About half-way through I stop, read what I have written, accept or change it, and get a feel for how much space I have left. Trained to write at this length, I feel I have all the room in the world left to discover what I have to say.

> And in saying that I realize that it may have been in the genes. I have a great-grandfather who emigrated from the Hebrides to begin a new life when he was 88. One grandfather had a "fiddle foot," he was always going off dancing to a new tune, a new enterprise, a new dream. So did my other grandfather, and my father kept changing jobs until he was in his seventies, always discontent.
>
> Their story was the story that lay under the new story I told myself when telling my friend the familiar story of my life. At my age, I have within me, layer upon layer of story, a mind that is like an archeological dig.
>
> I retold myself the story of my ancestors and the discontent that brought them from Scotland to New England. I would not, I had pledged when I was young, follow their path of discontent, chasing after rainbows that had no pot of gold.
>
> But of course I had, finding a wife who understood, or at least accepted, a husband who often scorned the publications he had accomplished, the awards he was given, because they were for the writing he did not intend to do but only the writing he had done.
>
> I look at my blank computer screen and relive, for a moment the private—and not so private—aching dissatisfaction that has rubbed raw almost all my adult life.
>
> I say aloud, "I have lived a life of discontent" and hear not guilt but pride for the first time. I want no Eastern, zen-like state of bliss, but the familiar Western itch to better myself, to get on, to do what probably can't be done.

> I realize, with a shock, that I have accomplished what I have done because I didn't want to do it but was driven toward another goal, a rainbow bending over the horizon.
>
> And telling myself—and you—this story I recognize the final irony: I am content with my discontent.

Three hundred and thirty-five words, seven hundred and fifty-four in all. I am home free. I will read it again and revise if it is necessary, but I realize that all through this draft the story was telling me about my life. In writing this short essay, I came to understand my heritage in a way I never had before, and I had come to accept and understand the way I had lived my own life as I never had before. The draft had revised me.

Revision After Drafting

When I was writing magazine articles I used to do three major drafts, reading and revising each ten times, thirty readings in all. That was in the days before computers and I would cross out and revise by hand, attaching inserts by tape or staple, producing long kite tails of drafts that Minnie Mae would type. Each of the three major revisions had its own focus.

Revision for content. I read the first draft to discover what I had to say, decide if it was worth saying and if I wanted to say it. There was no point in going on unless I knew what I was saying and was willing to say it. My meaning would be the North Star that would guide all other revisions. Often I would steal an idea from John Steinbeck and put what the article said in a single sentence. If I could not do that, I needed to revise. I also made sure I had the specific details that would satisfy the reader's hunger for information, the documentation that would support each point, and the examples that would clarify the message I had to deliver.

Revision for order. After I knew what I had said, I could order the information so that each word, each sentence, each paragraph drove the meaning forward. For years I cut the draft into individual paragraphs, rearranging them until I found a simple, clear line through the article, a sequence that answered the reader's questions at the moment they were asked.

Revision for language. This stage I would now call editing. I read aloud, line-by-line, tuning the voice to my meaning and my audience. The heard text that comes aloud in the reader's ear must be heard first by the writer.

In this draft, I paid close attention to everything in the text, checking each fact or citation for accuracy, making sure the spelling was correct, the attributions in place, the mechanics and rhetorical conventions broken only when they were essential to communicate or clarify meaning.

In recent decades, I find that I am doing all three readings or drafts simultaneously. But if I have difficulty with a piece I may break down my readings into that former sequence. I also find on the computer that I do all of them in chunks of writing or in my head as I write. My columns really are a first draft, as is this book—a first draft that is revised as it is written. The column that I have written is ready for editing although, as I have said above, the line between revising and editing overlaps.

Tricks of the Revision Trade

Each craft—baking or quilt making, pot throwing or gardening, cabinet making or antique restoration—has its own tricks. Here are some of the tricks I use in revising.

- I scan the draft, flying over the territory, to see if there are any large omissions.
- I read aloud to hear the music of the draft, making sure it communicates the meaning.
- I look for what works and develop that.
- I cut what can be cut. Less has always been more in my drafts.
- I ask the reader's questions and make sure they are answered.
- I consider the pace, slowing down the text so that the reader can absorb each point and speeding it up so the reader will not put it down.

I revel in the art of revision. I am rarely as happy as I am when I am crafting my text and therefore my life.

The Art of Editing

When you revise, you are your own reader. You revise, primarily, to discover, develop and clarify the subject for yourself. Now you become your own editor and clarify what you have written for your reader. You are your reader's advocate.

The Editing Attitude

To edit your own copy—or anyone else's—effectively, you have to have three levels of respect.

First of all, you have to respect the draft. Each piece of writing has its own integrity. The writer is not the creator but the midwife who assists the draft as it comes into the world. Each text has its own identity, and the editor has to cultivate it, making it clear to readers without turning it into something it is not.

As you edit your own copy, listen to the draft and follow it. It may have to be changed, but the draft is a rational product. It was produced by a process of thinking, of making intelligent choices. You may disagree with those choices, but first try to understand why they were made. The most unexpected turns in the draft, the ones that first look like errors or failures, even typos, may end up being the strongest points in the piece. Respect doesn't mean agreement. It doesn't mean leaving everything as it is. It means listening respectfully to the draft, considering the case the draft has made and then doing what has to be done.

Next you have to respect the writer. It is easy (normal, for me) to read my own draft and despair. It doesn't read as I expected; of course not. Writing changes in its writing. What is most strange, however, may be what is most important. Doris Lessing reminds us, "You have to remember that nobody ever wants a new writer. You have to create your own demand." Milan Kundera said, "To write a novel, you must be true to your obsessions, your ideas, and your imagination, and these are things with roots in your childhood. It is the images from your childhood and youth which form the imaginary country of your novels, and this imaginary country, in my case, is called Prague."

Be demanding of your own copy but on your own terms. Realize that every time you write you are developing your own voice, your own vision of the world, your own understanding of what that vision means. Respect yourself.

And also respect the reader. When I edit, I am the reader's advocate. I have been hired to represent the reader. I am no longer the author and have the responsibility to make sure my text speaks to someone other than myself.

There is great joy in editing. Now I have a draft that deserves close attention. I have a meaning, a form, abundant material, a focus and an order, a voice and I can, word-by-word, reveal the text.

There's nothing quite like the eagerness I feel when I sit down to edit. I will find out what I have said and, in making it clear to others, I will make it clear to myself. I will mark with a strikeout what I cut, insert new words in caps and add a commentary explaining what I have done and why. Join me as I edit the column, second- and third-guess me. I might edit it differently tomorrow: There is no single right way or wrong way.

> Driving down the highway, a young friend asks why I made the decision, at the age of 39, to come to the university and, as old men will, I told him more than he probably wanted to know.

I have a few strict rules. One of them is never, never ever begin a paragraph with a dependent clause and I can't remember having done it in years, but here it seems to catch a moment on the fly and establish the conversational tone of the essay. I'll keep it. I cut the comma after 39 and questioned "as old men will" but it seems to establish an appropriate discursive tone.

> Of course I wasn't so much telling him as telling myself in the hope of discovering a meaning or order I had not seen before. I confess what Minnie Mae knows only too well, that writers talk to listen to themselves. I "write" as I speak, telling a story I do not expect.

I feel guilty that I am not cutting but I read it over three times and feel each sentence pulls its weight. If I had to cut, I would take out the middle sentence but I think it sets up the last sentence in the paragraph and I think that sentence carries an idea that may be interesting to the reader.

> ~~At one level it MY STORY~~ THE STORY I TOLD was familiar, the lines worn with use~~, personal cliches I have told before~~: "When I was in college I wrote nothing but poetry, never worked on the college newspaper. I wanted to be a great poet but those jobs were taken WHEN I GRADUATED IN 1948."

I edited to make the paragraph simpler, to make it set up the quote but get to it faster.

> ~~I added a another familiar line, "I also wanted to be a great novelist but those jobs were also taken" and then I added a flourish, "I looked in the want advs. Nothing."~~

I was particularly proud of this paragraph yesterday for reasons I do not understand today. Cut.

> My friend seemed to nod in an encouraging manner. No matter, I would have gone on anyway. "I went to work on a newspaper because

> I wanted to write poetry, went to *Time* because they wanted me to be an editor and I wanted to write a novel, freelanced after I was fired by *Time*—they wanted to make me a TV producer—and freelanced magazine articles because I didn't want to write magazine articles."

I realize that my experience in writing fiction makes me break the story and bring in the listener. Having the listener there sets up what happens when I become my own listener a few paragraphs on. Of course, I didn't know I would continue the story when I drafted this paragraph, and I didn't know I would document what I had said in the beginning. The text knew but I didn't. Pay attention to the text. It will tell you what to write and how to write it.

> As my friend got out of the car at his house, I finished the story of my life. "I came to the university to teach journalism because I wanted to write fiction and poetry."
>
> He laughed and I went on telling my story to myself, how I wrote—and continue to write—books on writing and teaching because I want to write fiction and poetry.

I am simply filling out the story I know for the reader and the copy seems clean enough. I will not touch it.

> As I went down to my office, I feel the familiar old man's guilt that I hadn't done what I should have with my life, and I even heard my first wife's voice during a divorce more than 45 years ago saying that I was never content. I wanted to be out of college when I was in college, whatever I was doing I always wanted to be doing something else.

In writing this I confronted the monster I did not want to face and I heard a complaint from my first wife that I had not heard for decades. I needed to do this as the writer but do I need to share this with the reader? I decide I do, because readers will have their own monsters, their own old complaints from others in the past. It is essential to say this to set up what will come next.

> I sat before my computer and waited for the guilt. But it didn't come. I heard the new story that lay under the story I had told my friend. I had lived a life of discontent.

This is the turning point of the column. Unless I arrive at such a discovery I will not submit the column. I take the reader along on a voyage of discovery. We share the journey, and if we have no destination, I have no column. I questioned the story under the story, but it seems essential to what I am saying.

> And in saying that I realize that it may have been in the genes. ~~I have~~ A ~~a~~ great grandfather ~~who~~ emigrated from the Hebrides to begin a new life when he was 88~~. — Θ~~ ; one grandfather had a "fiddle foot," he was always ~~going off~~ dancing to a new ~~tune, a new enterprise, a new~~ dream; ~~So did my other grandfather and my~~ father kept changing jobs until he was in his seventies. ~~, always discontent.~~

I am surprised by the genetic discovery. It should have been obvious but it was not obvious to me before I wrote it. It was reason enough to write the piece. Now it has to be lined up more clearly for the reader. It was hard not to go on telling all the other stories of discontent but this was enough for the reader to establish the point.

> ~~Their story was the story that lay under the new story I told myself when telling my friend the familiar story of my life. At my age, I have within me, layer upon layer of story, a mind that is like an archeological dig.~~

This is difficult. It is a hard read but I think it is important. I have to read ahead to see if it can be cut or if I need to clarify it. *I can cut it and I can cut the first sentence of the following paragraph.*

> ~~I retold myself the story of my ancestors and the discontent that brought them from Scotland to New England.~~ I would not, I had pledged when I was young, follow their path of discontent, chasing after rainbows that had no pot of gold.
>
> But of course I had, finding a wife who understood, or at least accepted, a husband who often scorned ~~the~~ HIS publications, ~~he had accomplished, the~~ EVEN awards ~~he was~~ THEY WERE given, because they were NOT for the writing he ~~did not~~ intendED to do. ~~but only the writing he had done.~~

I return to the monster and to the wife mentioned above but I have to make the sentence run clear.

> I look at my blank computer screen and relive, for a moment the private—and no so private—aching dissatisfaction that has rubbed me raw almost all my adult life.

I might be able to cut this but I think it establishes the seriousness of my—and perhaps the reader's—neuroses.

> I say aloud, "I have lived a life of discontent" and hear not guilt but pride for the first time. I want no Eastern, zen-like state of bliss, but the familiar Western itch to better myself, to get on, to do what probably can't be done.

This had surprised me and I wondered in writing it if I were pushing it a bit much but it seems to run counter to a great deal of popular culture and therefore may add an interesting tension in the piece. It also seems to make me a member of another time, another generation, appropriate to a column called "Over 60."

> I realize, with a shock, that I have accomplished what I have because I didn't want to do it but was driven toward ~~another goal,~~ a rainbow bending over the horizon.

I always worry that I am telling the reader what to think in the end of a column. The essayist should make the reader think in the reader's own way, not instruct and therefore attempt to control the reader's thinking. I decide to keep the paragraph, partially to set up the last one.

> And telling myself—and you—this story I recognize the final irony: I am content with my discontent.

The seven hundred and fifty-four words before editing have shrunk to six hundred and twenty-seven, one hundred and twenty-seven words fewer than before but I think the content will expand in the reader's mind. Now I will submit it to Minnie Mae for her inspection and, if it passes, to Louise Kennedy at the *Globe.*

And since I started this section on editing with the concept of respect, I should end by saying I respect my editors. I am fortunate in having editors I can respect. It allows me freedom. When I have good editors I can try things I wouldn't dare if I knew my copy was going in as I had written it. I have had that situation and I have to be both the creator and the final censor. With good editors I can take a chance and they will tell me if it works—or does not work.

Do I accept what they suggest? More often than not. If they have a problem understanding the text, so will readers. My ego is greater than protecting the text. I believe that I can say what needs to be said in a hundred different ways so I listen to the editor and, more often than not, revise when there is a problem.

Tricks of the Editing Trade

Each writer develops techniques that work for the writer. My editing techniques include:

- I *hear* the draft, editing for the music of the text that will reveal and support its meaning.
- I play the devil's advocate, questioning the text, checking every fact, especially those that are so familiar I know without question they are accurate.
- I cut what can be cut, remembering the advice of Will Strunk as quoted by E. B. White. These words were over my writing desk for decades:

  > Vigorous writing is concise. A sentence should contain no unnecessary words, a paragraph no unnecessary sentences, for the same reason that a drawing should have no unnecessary lines and a machine no unnecessary parts. This requires not that the writer make all his sentences short, or that he avoid all detail and treat his subjects only in outline, but that every word tell.

- I edit with verbs and nouns, and with admiration for the subject-verb-object sentence.
- I imagine the flight of the sea gull and try to use the simplest word that will carry my meaning.
- The more complex the idea, the more important the information, the more likely I will write with short words, short sentences, short paragraphs.
- I am aware of the points of emphasis: most important at the end of a sentence, paragraph, section, piece, next-most important at the beginning and least important in the middle and make sure what should be emphasized is.
- I ask the reader's questions, and answer them immediately.
- I am aware of pace, the speed at which the reader is being carried through the text, and proportion, the size of each part of the text in relation to the other parts.
- Like the murderer, I try to erase my tracks. I remember George Orwell's statement, "Good writing is like a window pane." I want to call attention to my subject, not myself.

- While I am editing, George Orwell's list from "Politics and the English Language" always lurks in my memory (see page 59).
- I am a poor speller so I have a word book by my computer and use Spellcheck and Minnie Mae to make sure each word is spelled correctly.
- I'll put a piece of paper over the last sentence or paragraph. If I can read the piece and understand without that last piece of writing, then I move the paper up another paragraph. I keep doing that until I can't understand the poem, story, article, chapter without the covered paragraph. I did this on a novel and never published the last chapter in the final draft. The novel was finished before that chapter and, although I thought it was the best-written chapter in the novel, it was zapped.

Can you ruin a piece by revising and editing it too much? I haven't yet. It may happen, but not yet. I have kept revising so much I never finished a draft. I have a perfect beginning but no middle and no end, but I have found that even severe cuts—75 percent of the copy—strengthen the draft. Each revision and each editing goes to the center of what I have to say, and each time I make it better. Sometimes I stop when I discover nothing or no new way to say what I have written, but most of the time I stop revising and editing because I have a deadline.

Most writers become obsessed with getting it right and revise and edit too much. The danger is not that the writer will edit too little but edit too much. The writer has to let the draft go into the world, and that can be as hard (and essential) as letting a child go into the world.

Why Not Write a Book?

When beginning writers start talking about what they intend to write, I often say, "That's a book." A few have nodded and gone on to publish books but most are surprised—and terrified. They feel they should proceed modestly from short essay to extended essay, perhaps to nonfiction book; from anecdote to short story to novella to novel.

They do not realize that the novel is not a long short story and the nonfiction book is not an extended essay. Short story and novel, essay or article and nonfiction books are different genres, each with their individual traditions, problems, and potential.

Why Should I Write a Book?

It may be a lot easier to write a book than an essay or short story. In the shorter forms, the writer has to make skilled and sophisticated decisions that less is indeed more. It was harder for me to write a *Reader's Digest* story on the phonograph record business years ago than to write the juvenile nonfiction book I published on the same subject. I gathered almost the same amount of material, but the recording session, for example, that had to be shrunk to an anecdote for the article became a full chapter in the book. It is easier to write a chapter than to write an incident that implies all the material in a chapter.

In many ways it is more satisfying to write a book than an article or short story. When I write an article on an issue in teaching writing I limit the subject to what I know or want to know. When I wrote the first edition of *A Writer Teaches Writing*, my first textbook, I discovered I had to deal with issues that didn't particularly interest me, such as the role of grammar instruction in the writing course, as well as those that did interest me, such as the techniques of teaching revision. The writing of each textbook has forced me to learn even more than when I teach a course and can shape my syllabus to my own interests.

The writing of a book is, for me, an emotionally and intellectually satisfying experience. The dimensions of the book—fiction or nonfiction—give me daily problems of content and method to confront and solve. I have to think in writing, and I have to confront my own thinking.

I lose myself in the book, entering the page and living within the world of the draft. Writing a book stimulates me to weave together many threads from my life: I weave from memory and fantasy, from speculation and experience, from what I have read and what I have observed. My life becomes richer, fuller, more textured with each book I write or rewrite.

The book gives my life discipline. I have a daily task to perform within the evolving world of the book. When I leave my desk in late morning, my conscious and subconscious are doing the next morning's pages. I experience the comfort of habit, the familiarity of ritual, a certainty of expectation: I will, this morning, enter a situation in which I will do what I do not expect. I am confident of discovery.

The response to a book is also satisfying. People who will never read your book will be impressed by the accomplishment of writing a book. Those who read your books will be influenced by them over time, and they will be passed along to others who may pass them along to still others. They will last longer than a story in newspaper, magazine or journal.

Books will open doors to other books. Editors and publishers are interested in writers who have demonstrated the professional discipline to see a book through. Many who are given book contracts never complete them. If you have completed a book you are a member of a rather exclusive club.

When I did my first book I was surprised and delighted by the amount of control I had over the final draft. Newspaper and magazine editors had final control over my work, and most of the time I was not consulted as my work was rewritten, revised, and edited. When I did a book I became an author. Revisions were suggested, rarely commanded; I was expected to do my own rewriting; the final editing was even submitted for my approval.

But How Can I Write a Book?

A page at a time.

Write one page every morning and you have a 365-page book in a year. It is vital when writing a book to break the project down into daily tasks that can be accomplished under the realistic conditions of your life: working, parenting, housekeeping, cooking and eating, exercising, resting, relaxing.

In most cases, certainly in nonfiction books, this requires extensive planning. My nonfiction book planning is very specific. You will, of course, have to develop your own method based on your work style, the subject and type of book you are writing. Below are the steps I usually take.

Title. I work hard to get a title because that becomes the focal point for all the planning, researching, drafting, and consulting with editors that go into the making of a book. If I can reduce all the ideas I have about the book to a few words, it focuses my thinking, and this discipline of thought will be a positive force on all the rest of the planning and writing. I know the title may change radically along the way. This book was *Write to Teach Writing* through the first completed draft. It was a good title for a book on writing for teachers. When we decided this was a book for writers who may or may not be teachers, my editor, Tom Newkirk, suggested this title saying, "This is really what the book is about." *Crafting a Life in Essay, Story, Poem* became the title for the extensive revision—and cutting—of the manuscript. In both cases, I had the title in front of me as I wrote.

I may accept a title as I did from Tom because it was on target, but I usually draft dozens, even hundreds of titles, because each drafted title is an important thinking act, each is, in a way, a draft of a book

I may write with its own problems, solutions, content, design, purpose, voice, readership.

Table of contents. I revise the table of contents again and again, adding chapters, cutting others, dividing some, combining others, reordering them, making sure I have a title, not a label, for each section: "Why Not Write a Book" instead of "Book Writing." The title provides a discipline and focus for each chapter. I may write one to five lines introducing what is in the chapter or list the topics that will come under the chapter.

I share the table of contents with some writer friends to see what they think of my vision of the book and with the editor to make sure we are collaborating on the same book.

Preface. If I am writing a textbook, I draft the preface first. It reinforces the focus I have chosen for the working draft and, again, it allows the editor and the writer to reestablish their collective view of the work to be written.

The preface is of vital importance in a textbook because it is all most book salespersons have time to read. Their pitch to teachers who may adopt the book is based entirely on the points made in the preface.

On other books I do not like a preface. Few readers pay attention to anything that appears before Chapter One.

Chapters. I write the book by breaking it down into chapters and following a procedure that allows me to complete each chapter. Of course, some chapters break in half, others shrink to a section in another chapter or are eliminated; new ones appear as your discover the books; still others have to be moved forward and backwards, but the chapter is the principal building block of the book, and I follow the same sequence in writing each chapter.

Title. I reconsider and revise the title if it is necessary, narrowing and aiming the topic. The time I spend playing with the title is never wasted. This play-planning makes the rest of the work easier.

Lead. I write and rewrite the first sentence, the first paragraph, the first few paragraphs many times—a dozen, two dozen, three dozen, or more if needed. The first revisions usually approach the subject in different ways; the later revisions clarify and sharpen the approach I have chosen. Again, this is never time wasted—the voice, direction, and design of the chapter all grow out of the lead.

List. After writing the lead I often outline by making a quick list of what may follow. I find it more effective if I am specific, not writing "background" but "1st grade anecdote" or "what Newkirk did." The list may be scribbled in my daybook or on a 3" x 5" card, but usually it is written after the lead in the draft on the computer.

Sections. After the lead I may write the list in a more formal way, writing the subheads or section headings, as I did in this chapter, then filling in section by section. Of course, section heads disappear and others are added during the writing. If I cannot write a section easily I go on to the next one. At the end of the chapter I go back to the ones I have not written. About half of the sections don't need to be included in the book, the other half now come easily.

End. The final paragraph should echo the lead, imply a summary of the chapter but rarely summarize, and make the reader want to turn to the next chapter. To do all these tasks, the ending may have to be drafted a number of times—and then revised again and again.

Faith. The biggest problem in writing any book is keeping the faith and moving forward when everything makes you want to start over. There are times when you should start over but most of the time it is more important to press on, to get the book done so that it can be revised within its own evolved world.

Our faith in a book is usually severely tested a third of the way through and, again, two-thirds of the way through. I often have to keep myself going by dumb discipline. All writers suffer this lack of faith; published writers have written through the pages or weeks of doubt.

Find your own way to write your book but consider writing a book. Remember, a book is written the way everything else is written: one line at a time. You get this line right and that leads to the next and those lead to the next and . . .

Getting Published

Publication completes the act of writing that begins in private and ends in community. When we publish, we share what the writing has taught us and become a participant in the world in which we write. And, when I am published and receive a response to what I have written, I am stimulated to write. I am in the game.

There is no mystery about how writers get published: They submit their writing to editors. Some gets published, some does not. It is not a rational process but then, neither is life. I always tell beginning writers to get used to the idea that *acceptance is as irrational as rejection.* There is little to be learned from either acceptance or rejection, but publication only occurs when writers submit a manuscript to a publisher as many times as it takes to get published.

Here are my answers to the questions about getting published that I am most frequently asked.

When Should I Submit My Writing to an Editor?

As soon as possible. Set a deadline and meet it. Get on with the next piece of writing. Most beginning writers try to fiddle their drafts into perfection. There is no perfect draft. Send it out. Even if it is accepted it will probably have to be rewritten.

How Do I Know if a Draft Is Ready to Be Published?

You don't. That isn't your job, it is the editor's. And the editor certainly won't know unless you submit it.

Where Should I Send My Manuscript?

To the top market, the place you would most like to be published. There's no law that says you have to work up from a small magazine to a large one, a local publisher to an international publisher. Start at the top.

The best publishers will respond more quickly, provide better editing, pay more, establish your reputation, give you more readers.

Should I Study Magazines and Book Publishers to See What Is Being Published?

As long as you don't pay too much attention to them. Editorial policy decisions are made months or years before the issue you are reading is published and their policy may have changed. They may be looking for work that seems to contradict what is in the publication. Show your work. Remember what Doris Lessing said: "You have to remember that nobody ever wants a new writer. You have to create your own demand."

Do I Need an Agent?

No, not to find your first markets. After you have publishers interested in your work, you will be able to get an agent. Remember that the agent needs to be convinced you will produce enough writing year in and year out to help pay his or her rent in Manhattan or Hollywood. Never use an agent who advertises or charges a reading fee.

Should I Send the Same Manuscript to More Than One Editor?

Editors say "never," but editors take so long to make a decision that I find you can only get one response in the fall, perhaps one in winter if vacations don't interfere, another in the spring, rarely one in the summer. Acceptance is usually a committee decision, and it can take weeks for a committee to assemble and act.

If you do submit to more than one editor, do not tell them, and be prepared with a response if more than one accepts. In high school I once asked three girls to a dance, knowing none would say "yes." All three said "yes," all three knew each other. I became a joke and did not go to the dance. Figure out how to tell editors you prefer to publish with someone else.

When Should I Ask if They Have Made a Decision?

My rule of thumb is six weeks. If you inquire too early they can solve the problem by sending it back.

How Do I Convince an Editor That I Have the Authority to Write on This Subject?

The draft has to convince them.

You may, in a covering letter, say that you are an emergency-room nurse, a rural high-school teacher, a thrice-divorced mother of six if it is central to your story, but your authority must come from what you have said and how you have said it in the draft.

Should I Send a Manuscript or Write a Letter Asking if They Want to See It?

I work by query but if I have a written manuscript, I send it. A humor or mood piece can't be promised; the finished manuscript must sell itself.

If you have not written a manuscript but are selling an idea, the normal way to propose nonfiction articles and books is to write a proposal, called a *query*. I use the following form of the query.

```
Name
Address
including FAX or e-mail if you have them

                        TITLE
               by your writing name

The lead or first few paragraphs written as they
may appear in the final draft. The purpose of the
lead is to capture the editor's attention by
showing what a reader will see. Do NOT lecture
the editor, telling her what she should publish
or why. Reveal the prospective draft to her.
    Indent and list the three to five main points
the article will contain, telling the editor what
will support those points. I'd spend no more than
five lines each. In a nonfiction book proposal, I
would include a table of contents with chapter
titles that are lively and appropriate, followed
by indented statements averaging five lines that
tell the editor what will be covered in the voice
of the text.
    After you have listed the three to five main
points in an article or completed the proposed
table of contents, you may want to add any
information the editor needs to make a decision,
such as the fact you have access to police files
or you can draw on your experience as a nurse.
```

What Does a Professional Manuscript Look Like?

It is neat, easy to read and demonstrates a professional attitude. Normally your name and address are in the upper left hand corner of the first page in single space. The manuscript itself is double-spaced and numbered at the bottom center. It should never be stapled or bound in any manner but be held together by a paper clip or, in the case of a book manuscript, boxed.

Will They Read It?

Editors are hungry to find new writers, new voices, new approaches to familiar subjects. Editors rise on their ability to discover and cultivate new writers. They will read your manuscript, but they will scan it very quickly. It has to catch their attention immediately.

How Do You Get an Assignment?

By sending in a query or by being known because you have published something. It is not based on whom you know but what you have done and can do. Editors do not forget writers who deliver clean copy on deadline.

What Are My Chances of Getting Published?

Pretty good, if you keep manuscripts in the mail. Many well-known pieces of writing have been rejected ten, thirty, fifty times.

Should I Pay to Be Published?

No. Vanity presses exploit people and do not market or sell their books.

What Do You Wish You'd Known About Publishing When You Started?

That editors were looking for new writers.

How Do You Handle Rejection?

The pleasure of acceptance lasts a few moments, and then I am back at my desk, writing. Rejection lasts longer—perhaps ten minutes.

I have found that little is to be learned from rejection—it is not the writer that has been rejected but a piece of writing—and less is to be learned from acceptance—again, its not the writer that has been accepted but the writing. The reasons in both cases are mysterious and unimportant. Both rejection and acceptance should teach you that you must be yourself, the writer you cannot help being.

Acceptance and rejection are equally irrational, and the artist must learn to accept that. Both acceptance and rejection tell you more about the editor or award judge than the writer.

If you are wise, and I am not always wise, you write for yourself, write what you must write with respect for the evolving text, nurturing the draft, encouraging it toward its own meaning and its own audience.

Most of us know that it is impossible to raise a child in such a way as to guarantee that the child lives the life you wish you had led. It is the same with the text. The text has its own life and you must let it go.

The salvation is always the work. Following each morning's rejection or acceptance I do the same thing: write. My greatest satisfaction is to be lost in the writing.

Annotated Bibliography

Your Library of Craft

I remember the raw, gray winter afternoon after school when I hopped the trolley and rode to the great main library in Quincy Square and wandered through the stacks, looking for what I did not know. In the 800s section of the Dewey Decimal System, I found a book by Burton Rascoe, a long-forgotten Chicago newspaperman, who wrote of his experiences as a foreign correspondent.

It was 1938, I was fourteen years old, I knew I wanted to be a writer, and I discovered there were books that taught the publishing writer's craft, not the correctness I was taught in school but the art that allowed a story to rise from the page and be heard. I worked my way along the shelves of books by writers on writing and started writing down what they said, not knowing that I was following an old tradition and that many of the quotations from writers would be published in my own book, *Shoptalk—Learning to Write with Writers* (Boynton/Cook Publishers, Heinemann, Portsmouth, 1990).

For the past fifty-seven years I have continued to read books and articles on the writer's craft: writer's journals, letters, interviews, autobiographies, biographies and accounts of how they practice their craft. There is an enormous amount of testimony by writers on our craft and you should build your own library of craft with books and articles that take you into the workshops of other writers so that you can share the thoughts and feelings, problems and solutions of writers at work.

I have built my own library of craft by reading the first book I came across and then the one next to it and then the one that author mentioned, following my nose along the trail of the writers who come to their desks each morning, as I do, full of anticipation spiced with terror and give themselves up to the surprise of the page and lose themselves in the craft of making their discoveries clear to their readers.

Here are a few of the books on our craft that are on the shelves of my writing room where I can open them again and again as I continue my apprenticeship.

The Writing Life

Brande, Dorothea, *Becoming a Writer*, Harcourt Brace, New York, 1934; J. P. Tarcher, Los Angeles, 1981.

This book must have been one of the ones I found in 1938. My fingers remember holding this book and, in rereading it, I realize it has influenced all my work as a writer and a teacher of writing.

Dillard, Annie, *The Writing Life*, Harper & Row, New York, 1989.

An instructive and inspiring visit to the work room of a writer of fiction and nonfiction. She states and demonstrates many of the instincts and attitudes that lie behind the published works of writers.

Hall, Donald, *Life Work*, Beacon Press, Boston, 1993.

An extraordinary book by a poet who has written distinguished nonfiction that documents the habit of work—emphasize *work*. Writers write.

Jerome, John, *The Writing Trade—A Year in the Life*, Viking, 1992.

A candid, informative account by a nonfiction writer who instructs me by his skill. His classic *Stone Work* (Viking Penguin 1989) about building a stone wall is really a book on writing and I have given many copies of it to writer friends.

Lamott, Anne, *Bird by Bird—Some Instructions on Writing and Life*, Pantheon, New York, 1994.

The single best book for someone who wants to become a writer, because she anticipates the feelings of the beginning writer and responds to them.

Welty, Eudora, *One Writer's Beginnings*, Harvard University Press, Cambridge, 1984; Warner Books, 1985.

An instructive memoir by one of the finest writers of our time.

Conversations with Writers

Best Newspaper Writing—Winners of the American Society of Newspaper Editors Competition, edited by Roy Peter Clark, Don Fry, Karen F. Brown, Christopher Scanlan, Poynter Institute for Media Studies, St. Petersburg, annual editions 1979–1995.

These stories and the craft interviews with their writers are a major source of information on how journalists create literature under demanding limitations of time and space.

Sternburg, Janet, *The Writer on Her Work*, edited by Janet Sternburg, W. W. Norton, New York, 1980.

This collection is one of the best examples of the hundreds of such collections on my shelf and one I return to frequently. She has also published a second collection.

Writers at Work—Paris Review Interviews, Series I through IX, Viking Penguin, New York, 1958–1992.

I carry on a continuous conversation on craft with the best writers of our time, living and dead, through the enormous numbers of interviews with writers that have been collected in hundreds of books. Most of those books are in my library and they are, in fact, too numerous to mention. I think every serious writer should start a craft library by buying the entire series of interviews from the *Paris Review* and subscribing to the journal. These interviews are always perceptive and revealing and they now include an extraordinary number of the major writers of this century.

Writing Nonfiction

Barzun, Jacques and Graff, Henry F., *The Modern Researcher*, 3rd edition, Harcourt Brace, New York, 1977.

A classic that contains essential advice on the gathering of the information from which good nonfiction writing is constructed.

Huddle, David, *The Writing Habit: Essays*, Peregrine Smith Books/ GibbsSmith Publisher, Salt Lake City, 1991.

McPhee, John, *The John McPhee Reader*, editing by William Howarth, Random House, Vintage Books, New York, 1976.

The preface provides a revealing account of the working process of this nonfiction writer respected by all who practice our craft.

Rhodes, Richard, *How to Write*, Richard Rhodes, William Morrow, New York, 1995.

A detailed, thoughtful, and instructive book by an award-winning writer of nonfiction and fiction.

Zinsser, William, *On Writing Well*, by William Zinsser, HarperCollins, New York, 1990.

Perhaps the best book in print on the craft of writing, one that both beginners and professionals should study, because he both practices his craft and articulates his practice.

Writing Fiction

Afterwords: Novelists on Their Novels, edited by Thomas McCormack, Harper & Row, New York, 1969, St. Martins, New York, 1988.

Contains revealing accounts of novelists at work.

Burroway, Janet, *Writing Fiction—A Guide to Narrative Craft*, 4th edition, HarperCollins, New York, 1996.

One of the best textbooks on writing that grows richer and more valuable with each edition.

Forster, E. M., *Aspects of the Novel*, Penguin, New York, 1990.

A classic that should be read by anyone interested in writing narrative.

Greene, Graham, *In Search of a Character—Two African Journals*, Viking, New York, 1961.

A fascinating account of a novelist exploring the territories in which the distinguished novels *The Heart of the Matter* and *A Burnt-Out Case* will take place.

Hale, Nancy, *The Realities of Fiction: A Book About Writing*, Little Brown, Boston, 1962; Greenwood, 1977.

This wise book illuminated the geography of the fiction writer's world that I had not seen clearly until I read it.

Macauley, Robie and Lanning, George, *Technique in Fiction*, Harper & Row, New York, 1964.

A detailed exploration of the fiction writer's craft.

O'Connor, Frank, *The Lonely Voice: A Study of the Short Story*, World, Cleveland, 1963.

The best book on writing narrative by one of the best short story writers of the twentieth century because this master of narrative is able to show and tell the craft of fiction. I had an edition, now out-of-print, that included the complete text of each story he analyzed. It was borrowed and never returned.

Rule, Rebecca and Wheeler, Susan, *Creating the Story*, Heinemann, Portsmouth, 1993.
Two teachers of writing who practice what they preach explain the technicalities of narrative in an inspiring and disciplined way.

Steegmuller, Francis, *Flaubert and Madame Bovary: A Double Portrait*, Random House, Vintage Books, New York, 1939, 1950; University of Chicago Press, 1977.
One of the most fascinating books I have ever read—and reread. It is a detailed account of the making of a classic novel that has influenced us all.

Writing Poetry

Oliver, Mary, *A Poetry Handbook*, Harvest, 1994.
One of the most skilled poets of our age allows us to sit with her at her writing desk.

Wallace, Robert and Boisseau, Michelle, *Writing Poems*, 4th edition, HarperCollins, 1996.
I keep each edition of this book by my desk and turn to it for instruction and inspiration whenever the writing slows.

My Own Books

Years ago student members of the senate at the University of New Hampshire made a motion that would restrict professors from assigning their own books in their courses. The students were worried that the teachers would be paid for the course *and* receive royalties. I proposed that instructors be forced to assign their own books and face the students who had to read what they had written. I said I was worried about a teacher who would not stand behind what he or she had written. This book has evolved from all the writing I have done and especially from the books on writing and the teaching of writing that are still in print.

A Writer Teaches Writing, Houghton Mifflin, Boston, 1st edition 1968, 2nd edition 1985.
The first book I wrote trying to understand the writing process and how it might be taught. It is written for teachers and teachers of writing, and

not one line of the second edition came from the first. The first edition (1968) and second edition (1985) are entirely different books.

Learning by Teaching, Boynton/Cook Publishers, Heinemann, Portsmouth, 1st edition 1982, 2nd edition 1989.

The first collection of articles I published on writing and teaching writing.

Writing for Your Readers, Globe Pequot Press, Old Saybrook, 1st edition 1983, 2nd edition 1992.

Written for journalists, this book came directly from the work I did as a writing coach for the *Boston Globe* and other newspapers.

Write to Learn, Holt, Rinehart, Winston, 1st edition 1984, 2nd edition 1987, 3rd edition 1990; Harcourt Brace, Fort Worth, 4th edition 1993, 5th edition 1995.

A college text that has been used in elementary, middle, and high schools, it tries to define and explain the writing process. It is a basic book on writing that has evolved through each edition as my own writing and understanding of writing has evolved.

Read to Write, Holt, Rinehart, Winston, 1st edition 1985, 2nd edition 1990, Harcourt Brace, Fort Worth, 3rd edition 1993.

A reader that shows how many writers have used the writing process.

Expecting the Unexpected, Boynton/Cook Publishers, Heinemann, Portsmouth, 1989.

A second collection of articles documenting my exploration of the writing and teaching process.

Shoptalk, Learning to Write with Writers, Boynton/Cook Publishers, Heinemann, Portsmouth, 1990.

Perhaps my favorite book because it is so directly connected to the boy who dreamed of becoming a writer. It collects the best advice I could find on how to write easily and well.

The Craft of Revision, Holt, Rinehart, Winston, Fort Worth, 1st edition 1991, 2nd edition, 1994.

Writing is, of course, rewriting and these editions show how to rewrite early drafts so they may be published and read.

Writer in the Newsroom, Poynter Institute for Media Studies, St. Petersburg, 1995.

This is a copy of a talk on my lifetime apprenticeship and the reasons a writer should never burn out that I gave to journalists followed by an extensive interview and a complete bibliography of what I have written on the writing process.

Your library of craft will be different from mine, but your library and your bookstore will provide you with a continual flow of books that reveal the craft that must always be studied but can never be learned.